The

Everything You Need to Know

Copyright © 2023 by Noah Gil-Smith.

All rights reserved. No part of this book may be reproduced, distributed, or transmitted in any form or by any means, including photocopying, recording, or other electronic or mechanical methods, without the prior written permission of the publisher, except in the case of brief quotations embodied in critical reviews and certain other noncommercial uses permitted by copyright law. This book was created with the assistance of Artificial Intelligence. The content presented in this book is for entertainment purposes only. It should not be considered as a substitute for professional advice or comprehensive research. Readers are encouraged to independently verify any information and consult relevant experts for specific matters. The author and publisher disclaim any liability or responsibility for any loss, injury, or inconvenience caused or alleged to be caused directly or indirectly by the information presented in this book.

The Arctic Unveiled: An Introduction 6

A Frozen Past: Historical Discoveries 8

Arctic Explorers: Pioneers of the North 10

The Arctic Indigenous Peoples: Culture and Traditions 12

Arctic Geology: Understanding the Frozen Landscape 14

Polar Climate: The Secrets of Arctic Weather 16

Midnight Sun and Polar Nights: The Arctic's Unique Phenomena 18

Arctic Flora and Fauna: Wildlife Survival in Extreme Conditions 20

From Seal to Salmon: Arctic Cuisine Delights 22

Ice-Covered Oceans: Marine Life in the North 24

Glaciers and Icebergs: Majestic Arctic Giants 26

Polar Bears and Arctic Foxes: The Apex Predators 28

Arctic Birds: Migratory Wonders 30

Arctic Wildlife Conservation: Protecting the Fragile Ecosystems 32

Arctic Ocean Exploration: Unraveling the Abyss 34

Mysteries of the Aurora Borealis: Northern Lights Revealed 36

Chasing Ice: Climate Change in the Arctic 38

Indigenous Art and Crafts: Expressing Arctic Spirituality 40

Arctic Music and Dance: Rhythms of the North 42

Arctic Traditions: From Storytelling to Shamanism 44

Thule Culture: Ancient Arctic Societies 46

Arctic Architecture: Building in Extreme Environments 48

Languages of the North: From Inuktitut to Sami 50

Arctic Transportation: Navigating the Frozen Waters 52

The Northern Sea Route: Shipping in the Arctic 54

Arctic Policy and Governance: Balancing Interests 56

Greenland: The Land of Ice and Vikings 58

Svalbard: Norway's Arctic Gateway 60

The Faroe Islands: Where Nature Rules 62

Iceland: The Volcanic Heart of the Arctic 64

Nunavut: Canada's Arctic Frontier 66

Alaska: America's Last Frontier 68

Northern Russia: The Vast Arctic Expanse 70

Arctic Research Stations: Advancing Science in Isolation 72

Arctic Tourism: Experiencing the North Pole 74

Dogsledding and Snowmobile Safaris: Arctic Adventures 76

Glamping in the Arctic: Luxuries in the Cold 78

Arctic Cruises: Navigating Frozen Waters 80

Inuit Heritage Centers: Preserving Arctic Culture 82

Arctic Festivals: Celebrating Life in the Cold 84

Whaling in the Arctic: Tradition vs. Conservation 86

Arctic Mining: Resource Extraction in the North 88

Arctic Energy: The Quest for Oil and Gas 90

Arctic Diplomacy: International Relations in a Changing Climate 92

A Sustainable Future: Preserving the Arctic for Generations to Come 94

Epilogue 96

The Arctic Unveiled: An Introduction

Welcome to the majestic and enigmatic world of the Arctic, a region shrouded in icy allure and natural wonders. Nestled at the northernmost part of our planet, the Arctic remains one of the last frontiers of unexplored beauty. It stretches across approximately 14 million square kilometers, encompassing the Arctic Ocean, parts of eight countries, and countless islands. This vast expanse of frozen landscapes and frigid waters harbors an array of unique ecosystems, indigenous cultures, and breathtaking phenomena that have captivated explorers and adventurers for centuries.

At the heart of the Arctic lies the North Pole, the geographic center of the Arctic region. Surrounding this point is a frozen ocean covered by a floating ice cap, known as the Arctic ice pack, which undergoes seasonal fluctuations due to the changing temperatures. During the winter, the Arctic is cloaked in darkness as the region experiences polar nights, while in the summer, the sun never sets, leading to the phenomenon known as the midnight sun.

As you delve deeper into this frozen realm, you'll discover that the Arctic is not a monotonous white wilderness but rather a diverse mosaic of landscapes. Glaciers and icebergs, sculpted by millennia of freezing temperatures, dominate the coastal areas, while vast tundra plains, blanketed in mosses and lichens, spread across the interior. The Arctic is also adorned with mountain ranges, like the Brooks Range in Alaska and the Scandinavian Mountains in Norway, adding further to its captivating beauty.

Amidst the frozen expanses, the Arctic teems with life, exhibiting an incredible resilience to its harsh conditions. Numerous species have evolved unique adaptations to survive in this unforgiving environment. From polar bears, the apex predators of the Arctic, to agile Arctic foxes that change their fur color with the seasons, the wildlife here thrives in a delicate balance with their surroundings. The Arctic Ocean, too, is abundant with marine life, with beluga whales, narwhals, and walruses, amongst others, navigating through its frigid waters.

The Arctic also boasts a rich cultural tapestry, woven by its indigenous communities. For thousands of years, Arctic peoples, such as the Inuit, Yupik, and Sami, have lived in harmony with nature, relying on their deep knowledge of the land and its resources for sustenance and survival. Their customs, traditions, and art reflect a profound connection with the environment and a profound respect for its rhythms.

In more recent times, the Arctic has garnered global attention due to its rapidly changing climate. The region is experiencing some of the most severe effects of climate change, with temperatures rising at an alarming rate, leading to the melting of polar ice caps and the loss of habitat for its wildlife. These changes have significant implications not only for the Arctic itself but also for the entire planet, as they contribute to rising sea levels and impact weather patterns worldwide.

The Arctic is not an isolated enclave; rather, it plays a crucial role in shaping global climate and weather systems. Understanding the complex interactions within this ecosystem is vital for our collective efforts to mitigate climate change and preserve the delicate balance of our planet.

In the upcoming chapters of this book, we will embark on an expedition through the Arctic's history, delving into the stories of intrepid explorers who braved its icy frontiers. We will uncover the deep-rooted cultural traditions of the indigenous peoples and explore their artistic expressions. Together, we will witness the mesmerizing displays of the Northern Lights and learn about the significance of the midnight sun in the Arctic way of life.

Furthermore, we will examine the contemporary challenges faced by the Arctic, including environmental issues, resource exploitation, and geopolitical tensions among the nations that have a stake in this icy domain. As we navigate through these chapters, we will gain a comprehensive understanding of the Arctic's past, present, and the pressing issues shaping its future.

So, buckle up your parka and put on your snow boots as we embark on this incredible journey to unveil the Arctic's secrets and immerse ourselves in the beauty and complexity of this frozen realm. The Arctic awaits us with open arms, ready to share its wonders and mysteries as we explore its vastness and intricacies.

A Frozen Past: Historical Discoveries

In the annals of human history, the Arctic has remained a frozen frontier, beckoning explorers and adventurers to seek out its mysteries and secrets. From the early voyages of intrepid sailors to the modern scientific expeditions, the Arctic's past is a tapestry woven with tales of bravery, ambition, and the relentless pursuit of knowledge.

The first documented encounters with the Arctic date back to ancient times, when early civilizations like the Greeks and Romans speculated about a frigid land beyond their known world. It wasn't until the Viking Age (circa 8th to 14th century) that tangible evidence of Norse expeditions to the Arctic emerged. Viking sagas and historical records mention explorations to lands like Greenland and Vinland (likely modern-day Newfoundland), proving their remarkable seafaring prowess.

Fast forward to the Age of Exploration in the 15th and 16th centuries, and the Arctic emerged as a tantalizing goal for European navigators seeking a northern passage to Asia. Explorers like John Cabot, Martin Frobisher, and Henry Hudson ventured into the icy waters in search of the fabled Northwest Passage, a hypothetical sea route connecting the Atlantic and Pacific Oceans.

However, these early Arctic expeditions were fraught with peril. The harsh weather, treacherous ice conditions, and lack of knowledge about the Arctic's geography often led to tragic outcomes. Some ships were lost, and their crews met an uncertain fate in the unforgiving landscape. Nevertheless, these voyages laid the groundwork for future exploration and fueled the ambition to uncover the Arctic's secrets.

In the 19th century, a new era of Arctic exploration began, characterized by scientific endeavors and national rivalries. British explorers John Ross, William Edward Parry, and James Clark Ross made significant contributions to mapping the region and understanding its climatic conditions. Meanwhile, American explorer Elisha Kane and his expedition crew faced incredible hardships during their ill-fated search for the missing Franklin Expedition, which sought to find the elusive Northwest Passage.

It was during this time that the quest to reach the North Pole gripped the imagination of explorers worldwide. Notable figures like Robert Peary, Frederick Cook, and Roald Amundsen claimed to have achieved this remarkable feat, but controversy and conflicting evidence surrounded their claims, sparking debate that continues to this day.

One of the most tragic and iconic tales in Arctic exploration is that of Sir John Franklin's ill-fated expedition in 1845. Franklin, a seasoned British explorer, set out with two ships, the Erebus and the Terror, in search of the Northwest Passage. However, both ships became trapped in the ice, and the entire crew perished during their struggle to survive. The fate of Franklin's expedition remained a mystery until the mid-19th century when a series of expeditions led by John Rae, Francis Leopold McClintock, and Charles Francis Hall finally shed light on their tragic end.

The late 19th and early 20th centuries saw a surge in scientific exploration in the Arctic, with expeditions sponsored by various nations to study the region's geology, biology, and meteorology. These efforts laid the foundation for our understanding of the Arctic's unique ecosystems and their significance in the global climate system.

In 1909, Robert Peary's protégé, Matthew Henson, became the first African American to reach the North Pole, accompanying Peary on what is widely considered to be the first successful expedition to the Pole.

The race to the North Pole continued in the early 20th century, with American explorer Richard E. Byrd and Norwegian explorer Roald Amundsen both claiming to have reached the Pole by airship and airship, respectively, in the 1920s. However, these claims were met with skepticism, and the controversy surrounding the race to the Pole remains a subject of historical debate.

In more recent times, the Arctic has become a focal point for scientific research and international cooperation. Numerous research stations and observatories have been established across the region, allowing scientists to study climate change, monitor ice conditions, and understand the impacts of human activities on this delicate ecosystem.

Arctic Explorers: Pioneers of the North

The Arctic, with its frozen vastness and uncharted territories, has always beckoned daring souls to embark on daring expeditions in search of new frontiers and knowledge. These brave individuals, known as Arctic explorers, have left an indelible mark on history through their daring feats and contributions to our understanding of this remote region.

The roots of Arctic exploration can be traced back to ancient times when indigenous peoples, like the Inuit and Yupik, were the original explorers of the North. For thousands of years, they have traversed the Arctic's icy landscapes, hunting, fishing, and establishing trade routes. Their profound knowledge of the land and survival skills in extreme conditions laid the foundation for future Arctic explorers.

The European Age of Exploration in the 15th and 16th centuries marked the beginning of organized Arctic exploration by Western nations. Seeking a direct northern route to the riches of Asia, explorers like John Cabot and Martin Frobisher embarked on voyages to the Arctic, hoping to find the elusive Northwest Passage. However, these early attempts were met with disappointment as they faced treacherous ice conditions and hostile environments. In the 19th century, the quest for the Northwest Passage intensified, fueled by the promise of new trade routes and the prestige of conquering the icy wilderness. British Royal Navy officer Sir John Franklin led one of the most famous Arctic expeditions in 1845, with the Erebus and the Terror as his ships. Tragically, the expedition ended in disaster as both ships became icebound, and the entire crew perished. Numerous rescue missions and expeditions were launched to search for Franklin's lost crew, leading to further exploration and mapping of the Arctic.

It was during this period that other notable figures in Arctic exploration emerged. Elisha Kane, an American naval officer, led several expeditions in the 1850s and 1860s, attempting to locate Franklin's expedition and charting new areas of the Arctic. His harrowing accounts of survival and determination in the face of extreme conditions captured the imagination of the public and further fueled interest in Arctic exploration. In the late 19th and early 20th centuries, polar exploration saw new breakthroughs with the advent of advanced technologies and better understanding of polar conditions. Robert Peary, an American naval officer, embarked on multiple expeditions to the Arctic, culminating in his claim to have reached the North Pole in 1909. Peary's success was not without controversy, as there were doubts about the accuracy of his measurements and the possibility of reaching the exact geographic North Pole. Around the same time, Norwegian explorer Roald Amundsen became the first person to successfully navigate the Northwest Passage in 1906, achieving one of the greatest feats in Arctic exploration history. Amundsen's success demonstrated the viability of the passage for trade and further solidified the importance of Arctic exploration.

In 1926, the era of polar aviation began when American explorer Richard E. Byrd and his pilot Floyd Bennett claimed to have flown over the North Pole in an aircraft. However, their claim was later disputed, and questions arose about the veracity of their achievement. Despite the controversies, this milestone marked a turning point in Arctic exploration, with aviation becoming an essential tool for reaching remote and inaccessible areas. One of the most remarkable explorers of the Arctic was Fridtjof Nansen, a Norwegian scientist and diplomat. Nansen's innovative approach to Arctic exploration included deliberately trapping his ship, the Fram, in the ice to drift with the currents across the Arctic Ocean. This daring plan allowed him to collect valuable scientific data on ocean currents and ice movements. Although he did not reach the North Pole, Nansen's approach to polar exploration revolutionized scientific research in the region.

The mid-20th century saw a shift in Arctic exploration, with a focus on scientific research and international cooperation. Numerous research stations were established across the Arctic, facilitating groundbreaking studies on climate change, geology, and wildlife. Arctic explorers transformed into scientists, studying the region's delicate ecosystems and the impact of human activities on its environment. In recent times, Arctic exploration has continued to evolve, with a blend of scientific research, adventure tourism, and environmental conservation efforts. Modern Arctic explorers, equipped with advanced technology and knowledge, continue to push the boundaries of our understanding of this complex and changing region.

Throughout history, Arctic explorers have demonstrated incredible courage, resilience, and the indomitable spirit of human curiosity. Their exploits have not only expanded our knowledge of the Arctic but have also inspired generations to appreciate the beauty and fragility of this unique wilderness. As the Arctic continues to face challenges posed by climate change and human activities, the legacy of these pioneers of the North serves as a reminder of the importance of preserving and protecting this precious region for future generations.

The Arctic Indigenous Peoples: Culture and Traditions

In the frozen expanse of the Arctic, the land holds stories woven through generations of indigenous peoples who have inhabited this challenging environment for millennia. Their rich cultures and deep-rooted traditions have flourished in harmony with the harsh Arctic landscapes, leaving a profound impact on the region's history and shaping its present-day identity.

The Arctic is home to a diverse array of indigenous groups, each with their unique languages, customs, and ways of life. Among them are the Inuit, Yupik, Aleut, Saami, Nenets, and many others. These resilient communities have demonstrated remarkable adaptation to their surroundings, fostering a deep understanding of the land and its resources, which has been passed down through oral traditions and practical knowledge.

The Inuit, for instance, are widely recognized for their profound connection to the Arctic. With roots in Greenland, Canada, Alaska, and Chukotka (Russia), they have adapted to life in the extreme cold by crafting ingenious tools, such as the iconic kayak and umiak (skin-covered boat), for navigating icy waters. Their semi-nomadic lifestyle, centered around hunting marine mammals and fishing, reflects an intimate relationship with nature, where respect for animals and the environment is paramount.

In the northern reaches of Scandinavia, the Saami, also known as Laplanders, have maintained their reindeer herding traditions for centuries. The reindeer serve as their livelihood and cultural symbol, with the Saami's knowledge of the land and migratory patterns guiding their nomadic lifestyle. Their distinctive colorful clothing, adorned with intricate patterns, is a testament to their cultural heritage and sense of identity.

Across the Arctic, traditional hunting, fishing, and gathering practices continue to be integral to indigenous ways of life. The Yupik and Aleut peoples of Alaska, for instance, rely on hunting seals, whales, and fish for sustenance and cultural significance. They have developed an intimate understanding of their environment, knowing when and where to hunt and fish sustainably, respecting the delicate balance of the ecosystem.

The Nenets of the Russian Arctic are renowned for their reindeer herding traditions, similar to the Saami. Their semi-nomadic lifestyle revolves around the migration of reindeer herds, where the animals provide them with meat, milk, and materials for clothing and shelter. The Nenets' remarkable ability to navigate vast tundra landscapes with their reindeer is a testament to their resilience and deep cultural knowledge.

Language is a vital aspect of indigenous culture in the Arctic. Each group has its distinct language, reflecting their unique heritage and connection to the land. The Inuit, for instance, speak Inuktitut, while the Saami languages are part of the Uralic language family. Sadly, many of these languages are endangered, threatened by the encroachment of dominant languages and cultural changes.

Indigenous storytelling and oral traditions play a crucial role in passing down knowledge, history, and values from one generation to the next. These narratives recount the creation of the world, the relationship between humans and nature, and the customs that govern community life. Through storytelling, indigenous peoples preserve their cultural heritage and maintain a strong sense of identity in a rapidly changing world.

Cultural practices and ceremonies in the Arctic often center around significant life events, such as births, marriages, and deaths. These rituals are deeply spiritual and demonstrate a profound respect for the interconnectedness of all living beings and the natural world. Mask dances, drum ceremonies, and feasts are just a few examples of these cultural expressions, where the entire community participates and celebrates its heritage.

In modern times, the Arctic's indigenous peoples face a range of challenges, including the effects of climate change, resource exploitation, and the erosion of traditional knowledge. Despite these challenges, they continue to play a vital role in advocating for environmental conservation, indigenous rights, and cultural preservation.

Indigenous organizations and initiatives work tirelessly to revitalize and protect their languages, arts, and traditional practices. Collaborations with scientists and researchers have resulted in valuable insights into Arctic ecosystems and climate change, emphasizing the importance of combining traditional knowledge with modern science.

Arctic Geology: Understanding the Frozen Landscape

Beneath the pristine ice and snow of the Arctic lies a geological tapestry that holds clues to the Earth's history and processes that have shaped this frozen expanse over millions of years. Arctic geology is a captivating field of study, revealing the complex interactions between the land, ice, and the ocean in this unique and harsh environment.

At the heart of the Arctic's geology lies the Greenland Ice Sheet, an immense ice mass covering about 1.7 million square kilometers – roughly three times the size of Texas. This massive ice sheet is the second-largest in the world, surpassed only by the Antarctic Ice Sheet. It holds an astonishing 10% of the world's freshwater, a testament to the colossal scale of ice accumulation over millennia.

The Greenland Ice Sheet is not a static feature; it moves, shifts, and flows, responding to changes in temperature and snowfall. Glaciers, which are vast rivers of ice formed from compacted snow, form the arteries of the ice sheet, carrying ice from the interior to the edges, where it calves off as icebergs into the ocean. This dynamic ice flow plays a crucial role in shaping the Arctic's landscapes, carving out deep fjords and valleys in coastal regions.

Beyond Greenland, the Arctic is also home to numerous ice caps, smaller ice masses covering individual mountains or plateaus. These ice caps, along with the vast Arctic ice pack, contribute to the overall stability and fragility of the region's ice.

Beneath the ice, the Arctic's geological history is inscribed in its bedrock. The region's rocks tell the story of ancient continental collisions, volcanic activity, and the ebb and flow of ancient oceans. Geologists have identified a series of geological provinces within the Arctic, each with its unique characteristics and history.

The Canadian Shield, for example, spans much of northern Canada and Greenland, comprising some of the oldest rocks on Earth, dating back billions of years. This ancient and stable geological province has played a critical role in shaping the landscapes we see today, with erosion and glaciation leaving their marks on the terrain.

The Arctic also hosts significant oil and gas reserves, with the Barents Sea off the coast of Norway and Russia holding substantial hydrocarbon resources. As the ice retreats due to climate change, these resources become more accessible for exploration and exploitation, sparking debates over environmental conservation and energy security.

Volcanic activity has also played a role in shaping the Arctic's geology. Iceland, situated on the Mid-Atlantic Ridge, is one of the most volcanically active regions in the world. The island's geothermal energy resources provide an essential source of power and heat for its inhabitants, serving as a sustainable alternative to fossil fuels.

Tectonic forces continue to shape the Arctic, as evidenced by the ongoing opening of the Arctic Ocean's Lomonosov Ridge due to seafloor spreading. This geophysical process, driven by the movement of Earth's tectonic plates, adds to the complexity of the Arctic's geological dynamics.

Arctic geologists study the region's permafrost, the layer of permanently frozen ground that covers about a quarter of the Earth's land area. The thawing of permafrost due to rising temperatures has significant implications for the region, leading to ground subsidence, landslides, and the release of greenhouse gases trapped within the frozen soil.

In recent years, advances in technology and remote sensing have revolutionized Arctic geology research. Satellite imagery and ground-penetrating radar provide valuable insights into the ice sheet's movement and the underlying geology. Moreover, ice cores drilled from the ice sheets offer a unique window into the Earth's climate history, revealing past atmospheric conditions and greenhouse gas concentrations.

Polar Climate: The Secrets of Arctic Weather

In the Arctic, the weather is an ever-changing dance of extremes, where icy winds and frigid temperatures dominate the landscape. The polar climate of the Arctic is a marvel of meteorological wonders, shaped by its unique position near the North Pole and the interplay of various atmospheric forces.

At the heart of the Arctic climate lies the polar cell, a large atmospheric circulation pattern that forms due to the temperature difference between the equator and the pole. The polar cell plays a critical role in determining the region's weather patterns, driving the circulation of air masses and the formation of weather systems.

During the winter months, the Arctic experiences polar nights, a phenomenon where the sun remains below the horizon for an extended period. This lack of sunlight leads to prolonged darkness and bitterly cold temperatures, often plunging well below freezing. The absence of sunlight also limits the warming of the land and sea, further reinforcing the cold conditions.

Conversely, the summer months bring the midnight sun, an enchanting spectacle where the sun remains visible 24 hours a day. The constant daylight warms the Arctic, melting ice and snow, and giving rise to a short-lived burst of life and activity. While summer temperatures are relatively milder, they seldom reach the levels experienced in lower latitudes due to the persistent presence of ice and snow.

The Arctic's proximity to the North Pole results in unique atmospheric phenomena, such as the Arctic oscillation (AO) and the North Atlantic Oscillation (NAO). These atmospheric oscillations influence the position and strength of the polar jet stream, which, in turn, affects the track of weather systems and storm patterns.

In recent years, the Arctic has been experiencing significant changes in its climate due to global warming. The region is warming at a rate more than twice as fast as the global average, leading to the accelerated melting of sea ice and glaciers. This phenomenon, known as Arctic amplification, has far-reaching consequences for the Arctic ecosystem and global climate.

The melting of Arctic sea ice affects weather patterns beyond the polar region. The loss of ice reduces the amount of sunlight reflected back into space, leading to increased absorption of solar energy by the darker ocean waters. This process contributes to the warming of the oceans and the atmosphere, further amplifying the effects of climate change.

As the Arctic warms, the delicate balance of the region's climate is disrupted. The shrinking ice cover affects the habitat of Arctic wildlife, from polar bears and seals to migratory birds. The thawing permafrost releases methane and carbon dioxide, potent greenhouse gases that contribute to the greenhouse effect and global warming.

The Arctic's complex climate interactions have far-reaching consequences for the rest of the world. Changes in the polar jet stream can influence weather patterns in the mid-latitudes, leading to extreme weather events like heatwaves, storms, and prolonged droughts. The melting of Arctic ice also contributes to rising sea levels, posing risks to coastal communities worldwide.

Understanding the intricacies of Arctic weather is essential for predicting and mitigating the impacts of climate change. Scientists and researchers continually study the region's climate patterns, gathering data from weather stations, satellites, and ice cores to unravel the secrets of the Arctic's meteorological mysteries.

The Arctic's climate is a delicate dance of ice and air, where each shift in temperature, wind, and pressure contributes to a finely balanced ecosystem. As climate change continues to reshape the region, the secrets of Arctic weather become ever more critical to grasp. The future of the Arctic and the global climate are intrinsically linked, making it crucial for us to protect and preserve this frozen frontier for generations to come.

Midnight Sun and Polar Nights: The Arctic's Unique Phenomena

In the enchanting realm of the Arctic, where the frigid landscape meets the endless horizon, two mesmerizing phenomena reign supreme – the Midnight Sun and the Polar Nights. These awe-inspiring events are a testament to the Arctic's unique position on Earth, where its proximity to the North Pole shapes the passage of time and the dance of light and darkness.

During the summer months, the Arctic experiences the Midnight Sun, an extraordinary spectacle that captivates both locals and visitors alike. As the Earth tilts on its axis, the Arctic region tilts towards the sun during the summer solstice. This means that for a period, often lasting several weeks, the sun never sets below the horizon, casting its radiant glow across the Arctic landscape, day and night.

Imagine a world where the sun remains suspended in the sky, casting shadows that shift but never quite disappear. In this surreal experience, time seems to lose its usual meaning, and the natural rhythms of life are transformed. The Midnight Sun has a profound impact on the Arctic ecosystem, awakening dormant plants and animals and sparking a flurry of activity in the brief window of warmth and light.

For the indigenous peoples of the Arctic, the Midnight Sun holds great cultural significance. It marks a time of abundance, when the land teems with life, and hunting and fishing become bountiful. Festivals and celebrations are held to honor the sun's presence, and traditional ceremonies are performed to express gratitude for the gifts it bestows upon the people.

As the summer days stretch on, the Arctic begins its gradual tilt away from the sun, and the transition to the Polar Nights begins. As autumn arrives, the days grow shorter, and the sun dips lower on the horizon. The Polar Nights signal the approach of winter, bringing a profound change to the Arctic's landscape and climate.

During the winter solstice, the Arctic region is plunged into darkness as the sun disappears below the horizon for an extended period. This phenomenon, known as the Polar Nights, can last for several weeks, with the degree of darkness varying depending on the latitude. Near the North Pole, the Polar Nights can extend for months, creating a world cloaked in perpetual darkness.

The Polar Nights present a stark contrast to the Midnight Sun, plunging the Arctic into an otherworldly silence and stillness. Yet, even in the depths of darkness, the Arctic does not lose its allure. Instead, it transforms into a canvas for celestial wonders. The Northern Lights, also known as the Aurora Borealis, paint the Arctic sky with breathtaking displays of dancing colors, adding a touch of magic to the Polar Nights.

The Polar Nights present unique challenges for those who call the Arctic home. Inhabiting a land shrouded in darkness for an extended period requires resilience, adaptation, and a deep understanding of the rhythms of nature. Indigenous communities, such as the Inuit and Saami, have thrived in the Arctic for generations, relying on their knowledge of the land and the stars to navigate and survive during the Polar Nights.

The Midnight Sun and the Polar Nights are not just awe-inspiring phenomena; they are also crucial to understanding the Arctic's role in the global climate system. The extended periods of sunlight during the summer contribute to the warming of the region, influencing ice melt, permafrost thaw, and Arctic ecosystems. Likewise, the extended darkness during the Polar Nights impacts the region's temperatures and ecological dynamics.

As climate change continues to affect the Arctic, the rhythms of the Midnight Sun and the Polar Nights are also shifting. The timing and duration of these phenomena are evolving, posing new challenges for the delicate balance of Arctic ecosystems and the way of life for its inhabitants.

The Midnight Sun and the Polar Nights are the Arctic's celestial storytellers, narrating the cyclical dance of light and darkness that shapes this extraordinary region. They are a reminder of the Arctic's uniqueness and the delicate interplay between the Earth, sun, and its frozen landscapes.

Arctic Flora and Fauna: Wildlife Survival in Extreme Conditions

In the vast and frozen expanse of the Arctic, life flourishes in the face of extreme conditions. Arctic flora and fauna have adapted over millennia to survive in one of the harshest environments on Earth, where temperatures plummet far below freezing, and the land is often blanketed in ice and snow.

Let's start with the plant life of the Arctic. Despite the challenging conditions, various plants have carved out niches in this icy wilderness. The Arctic tundra, characterized by low temperatures and a short growing season, supports hardy vegetation, such as mosses, lichens, and dwarf shrubs. These plants are adapted to withstand freezing temperatures and strong winds, growing close to the ground to conserve heat and minimize exposure to the elements.

One of the most iconic plants of the Arctic is the Arctic poppy (Papaver radicatum). Its vibrant yellow flowers dot the tundra during the brief summer, providing a burst of color amidst the otherwise stark landscape. The Arctic poppy's ability to bloom in such adverse conditions is a testament to its resilience and adaptability.

Another vital component of Arctic plant life is the lichen. Lichen is a symbiotic relationship between fungi and algae or cyanobacteria. These hardy organisms cover vast expanses of the Arctic tundra, providing food and shelter for various animals. Lichen is particularly crucial for herbivorous animals like reindeer, muskoxen, and Arctic hares, which rely on it as a primary food source.

In the Arctic Ocean, the underwater world teems with life. The icy waters are home to a diverse array of marine creatures, from microscopic plankton to colossal whales. Seals, such as the ringed seal and the bearded seal, are abundant in the Arctic, thriving in icy waters and using their specialized bodies to navigate through the ice.

The Arctic's most iconic animal is undoubtedly the polar bear (Ursus maritimus). As the apex predator of the Arctic, polar bears have adapted to hunt and survive in the frozen landscapes. They are powerful swimmers, capable of covering vast distances in search of food and suitable habitats. Their thick layer of blubber and dense fur provide insulation against the extreme cold, making them uniquely suited to the Arctic's icy waters.

Polar bears primarily feed on seals, relying on the ice to hunt for their prey. However, the rapid loss of sea ice due to climate change poses a significant threat to their survival. With less ice available, polar bears have to swim longer distances to find food, leading to increased energy expenditure and diminished reproductive success.

Another remarkable Arctic predator is the Arctic fox (Vulpes lagopus). The Arctic fox's exquisite white coat serves as camouflage in the snowy landscape during the winter, changing to a darker color in the summer. These clever creatures are skilled hunters and scavengers, able to find food even in the harshest conditions.

For many Arctic animals, the summer is a time of plenty, when the ice melts, and food becomes more accessible. During this brief period, birds flock to the Arctic to breed and raise their young. The Arctic tern, known for its remarkable migration, travels all the way from the Arctic to the Antarctic and back each year, making it one of the world's most well-traveled birds.

Marine mammals, such as whales, walruses, and narwhals, also make their way to the Arctic during the summer. The region's rich waters provide them with abundant food sources, making it a crucial feeding ground for these majestic creatures.

The survival of Arctic flora and fauna relies on their ability to adapt to the changing conditions. Climate change poses a significant threat to their existence, as the loss of sea ice, rising temperatures, and alterations in food availability challenge their delicate balance. Protecting the Arctic ecosystem and its wildlife is crucial for maintaining biodiversity and understanding the broader impacts of climate change on our planet.

From Seal to Salmon: Arctic Cuisine Delights

In the Arctic, where survival hinges on ingenuity and resourcefulness, the cuisine reflects the rich diversity of the region's natural bounty. Arctic cuisine is a delightful tapestry of flavors, shaped by the traditions of indigenous peoples and the availability of ingredients in this challenging environment.

One of the primary sources of sustenance in the Arctic is the sea, teeming with an abundance of marine life. Seal meat has been a vital food source for Arctic indigenous communities for thousands of years. The Inuit and other Arctic peoples have long relied on seals for their meat, blubber, and skin, using every part of the animal in a practice known as "ayaya" or "respectful hunting." Seal meat is rich in nutrients and provides essential vitamins and proteins necessary for surviving the harsh Arctic climate.

Salmon is another prized culinary treasure of the Arctic. As the Arctic rivers come alive with the arrival of summer, salmon swim upstream in massive numbers to spawn. This annual spectacle not only sustains local communities but also attracts fishermen from afar, eager to partake in the rich salmon harvest. Salmon is often smoked, dried, or prepared in various traditional dishes, making it a staple in Arctic cuisine.

Reindeer meat holds a special place in the culinary traditions of the Saami and other Arctic communities. Reindeer herding is an essential aspect of their way of life, and the animals provide sustenance in the form of tender venison and rich gamey flavors. The Saami skillfully prepare reindeer meat, using various traditional cooking methods to create hearty and flavorful dishes.

The Arctic's coastal regions offer an abundance of seafood, with fish such as Arctic char, cod, and halibut playing prominent roles in the diet of coastal communities. The Arctic char, a member of the salmon family, is prized for its delicate taste and high nutritional value. Its pink flesh, similar to that of salmon, is a delicacy often prepared in various ways, from grilling to curing.

Berries are a cherished part of Arctic cuisine, providing a burst of flavor and a dose of essential vitamins. Wild berries, such as cloudberries, blueberries, and crowberries, grow abundantly in the Arctic tundra during the summer months. These vibrant gems are often used to make jams, sauces, and desserts, infusing Arctic dishes with natural sweetness and color.

In modern times, traditional Arctic cuisine has been complemented by imports and influences from other regions. Communities near the Arctic Circle now have access to a broader range of food items through trade and transportation. However, the traditional culinary practices and knowledge of preparing Arctic delicacies continue to be passed down through generations.

The preparation of Arctic cuisine is as much about preserving cultural heritage as it is about nourishing the body. Traditional cooking methods, such as smoking, drying, and fermenting, allow food to be stored for long periods, ensuring a steady food supply during the harsh winters.

In recent years, there has been a growing interest in Arctic cuisine beyond the region's borders. Arctic-inspired dishes, with their focus on local and sustainable ingredients, have captured the attention of food enthusiasts and chefs worldwide. This newfound appreciation for Arctic flavors brings attention to the region's unique culinary heritage and the importance of preserving traditional food knowledge.

As climate change poses challenges to the Arctic ecosystem, including shifts in traditional food sources and access to marine resources, the preservation of Arctic cuisine takes on added significance. Sustainable practices, respect for nature, and responsible harvesting of resources are essential in ensuring the continuation of Arctic culinary delights for generations to come.

From seal to salmon and everything in between, Arctic cuisine reflects the resilience and resourcefulness of the people who have thrived in this challenging environment for centuries. With every savory bite and vibrant flavor, Arctic cuisine tells a story of survival, culture, and appreciation for the extraordinary beauty of this frozen frontier.

Ice-Covered Oceans: Marine Life in the North

In the northern reaches of our planet, the Arctic Ocean stands as a vast and ice-covered realm, teeming with marine life that has evolved to thrive in some of the harshest conditions on Earth. The icy waters and shifting sea ice create a unique ecosystem, supporting an array of fascinating creatures that have adapted to the challenges posed by the frigid environment.

At the heart of the Arctic marine ecosystem is the sea ice itself. This ever-changing frozen landscape serves as both a habitat and a crucial part of the Arctic food web. Underneath the ice, algae and phytoplankton grow, providing the foundation of the Arctic's marine food chain. These microscopic organisms serve as food for zooplankton, which, in turn, become sustenance for larger animals like Arctic cod, herring, and other small fish.

Arctic cod, also known as polar cod, play a significant role in the Arctic ecosystem. They are essential prey for various marine predators, including seals, seabirds, and larger fish like the Greenland shark. The Greenland shark, a cold-water species found throughout the Arctic and North Atlantic, can reach enormous sizes and is one of the region's apex predators.

One of the Arctic's most iconic inhabitants is the polar bear. While polar bears are often associated with the land, they are excellent swimmers, and much of their life is spent on the sea ice. They rely on the ice to hunt seals, their primary food source, by patiently waiting near breathing holes or using their powerful swimming skills to reach seals resting on the ice. As sea ice diminishes due to climate change, the challenges for polar bears in finding food and suitable habitats increase, posing a significant threat to their survival.

Seals, including the ringed seal, bearded seal, and harp seal, are other essential members of the Arctic marine community. These marine mammals spend much of their lives in and around the icy waters, using the sea ice as platforms for resting, breeding, and giving birth. For many Arctic indigenous communities, seals have been a vital food source and a crucial part of their cultural heritage for generations.

Beluga whales are a common sight in the Arctic, known for their distinctive white color and melodic vocalizations. Belugas are incredibly social animals and often travel in groups, making them a delight for researchers and tourists alike. The Arctic's rich waters provide these whales with abundant fish and invertebrates to sustain their diet.

The narwhal, often referred to as the "unicorn of the sea," is another remarkable inhabitant of the Arctic waters. Male narwhals boast a long, spiral-shaped tusk, which is actually an elongated tooth. The function of this unique appendage remains a subject of scientific study and speculation, but it is believed to play a role in communication and mating rituals.

Birds are also integral to the Arctic marine ecosystem, with various species making their way to the Arctic to breed and raise their young during the summer. The Arctic tern, famous for its extraordinary migration, travels from the Arctic to the Antarctic and back each year, covering thousands of miles. Other seabirds, such as guillemots, puffins, and fulmars, also rely on the Arctic's abundant fish populations to sustain their colonies.

The Arctic's marine life has adapted to the seasonal changes and extreme conditions, taking advantage of the short but intense summer to feed and reproduce. During the long winter months, many marine animals migrate or adjust their behavior to cope with the darkness and freezing temperatures. The sea ice itself serves as a critical habitat for various species, from plankton to mammals, offering a place to rest, breed, and find food.

Climate change poses significant challenges to the Arctic marine ecosystem. As the sea ice melts and the region warms at an accelerated rate, the delicate balance between species and their habitats is disrupted. Marine animals face changes in the availability of food, shifts in migration patterns, and increased competition for resources.

Understanding and preserving the Arctic marine ecosystem is vital not only for the creatures that call it home but also for the health of our planet. The Arctic Ocean plays a crucial role in regulating the Earth's climate, and its marine life serves as a barometer for the impacts of global warming. Conservation efforts, sustainable fishing practices, and responsible management of the Arctic's resources are essential to ensure the continued existence of its vibrant marine life for generations to come.

Glaciers and Icebergs: Majestic Arctic Giants

In the Arctic, immense glaciers and icebergs stand as awe-inspiring symbols of the region's frozen grandeur. These colossal ice formations have shaped the landscape for thousands of years, leaving their mark on the Earth's history and captivating the imagination of all who encounter them.

Glaciers are massive rivers of ice, formed from compacted snow and ice that accumulate over centuries. They flow slowly downhill under their own weight, carving out valleys and fjords as they inch their way towards the sea. The Greenland Ice Sheet, one of the most significant glaciers in the world, covers about 80% of Greenland's landmass and holds an astonishing volume of ice. It's hard to fathom the sheer scale of this ice sheet, which is roughly three times the size of Texas.

As glaciers reach the ocean, they give birth to another Arctic wonder – icebergs. These magnificent ice structures break off from the glaciers and float freely in the Arctic waters. While icebergs appear massive above the water's surface, only about one-tenth of their mass is visible, with the majority submerged below the surface.

Icebergs come in various shapes and sizes, each an ephemeral work of art sculpted by nature. Some icebergs are towering and jagged, resembling frozen skyscrapers, while others have smooth curves and serene beauty. The colors of icebergs can range from brilliant white to mesmerizing shades of blue, created by the compression of ice and the scattering of sunlight.

The movement of icebergs in the Arctic is both graceful and unpredictable. Driven by ocean currents and winds, icebergs can travel thousands of miles from their point of origin, often lingering for weeks or months before eventually melting away. Some icebergs become temporarily grounded in shallow waters, creating ice mosaics that add to the Arctic's ever-changing tapestry.

One of the most famous icebergs in the Arctic is the Petermann Ice Island, which calved off the Petermann Glacier in Greenland. This enormous iceberg made headlines when it broke away, capturing the world's attention as it drifted into the North Atlantic.

While icebergs may appear to be silent giants, their movements can have significant impacts on the Arctic environment. As they drift into warmer waters, icebergs can release freshwater into the ocean, affecting salinity levels and influencing ocean circulation. Their melting can also contribute to sea-level rise, making them important components of the global climate system.

The calving of icebergs from glaciers is a natural process, but it has been accelerating in recent years due to climate change. Rising temperatures in the Arctic lead to increased ice melt, causing glaciers to retreat at an alarming rate. The loss of glacial ice contributes to rising sea levels and has far-reaching implications for coastal communities around the world.

Glaciologists and researchers study Arctic glaciers and icebergs to understand their behavior and the impacts of climate change on these majestic ice formations. Advanced technologies, such as satellite imagery and ice-penetrating radar, allow scientists to monitor glacial changes and assess their contribution to global sea-level rise accurately.

In the face of rapid climate change, the Arctic's glaciers and icebergs remind us of the urgency to protect and preserve our planet's delicate ecosystems. These frozen giants are not only symbols of natural beauty but also important indicators of the Earth's changing climate.

Polar Bears and Arctic Foxes: The Apex Predators

In the Arctic, where survival is a constant battle against the elements, two remarkable predators reign supreme – the polar bear and the Arctic fox. These apex predators have honed their skills and evolved over thousands of years to become masters of the frozen wilderness.

The polar bear (Ursus maritimus) stands as the undisputed king of the Arctic. As the largest land carnivore on Earth, polar bears are perfectly adapted to their icy habitat. Their thick layer of blubber and dense fur provide insulation against the extreme cold, enabling them to swim and hunt in frigid waters for extended periods.

Polar bears are highly skilled swimmers, capable of covering vast distances in search of food. Their preferred prey is the seal, which they catch by waiting near breathing holes or using their powerful swimming skills to reach seals resting on the ice. These intelligent hunters can also detect seals beneath the ice using their acute sense of smell.

During the summer months, when the sea ice retreats, polar bears face challenges in finding food. With less ice available, they have to swim longer distances to locate prey, leading to increased energy expenditure. As climate change accelerates the melting of Arctic sea ice, the survival of polar bears becomes increasingly uncertain, making them one of the most vulnerable species to global warming.

The Arctic fox (Vulpes lagopus), on the other hand, is a versatile and resourceful predator. This small but tenacious creature has adapted to thrive in the Arctic's harsh conditions. The Arctic fox's exquisite white coat serves as camouflage in the snowy landscape during the winter, changing to a darker color in the summer to blend in with the tundra.

Arctic foxes have an omnivorous diet, feeding on a variety of foods, including small mammals, birds, eggs, and even plant matter. During the lean winter months, when prey is scarce, they have the remarkable ability to store excess food and cache it under the snow, creating hidden stashes that they can rely on during times of scarcity.

One of the Arctic fox's most intriguing behaviors is its ability to follow in the footsteps of polar bears. When polar bears hunt seals and leave behind the carcasses, Arctic foxes are quick to scavenge the leftovers. This opportunistic behavior allows the Arctic fox to capitalize on the polar bear's successful hunts, ensuring a steady food supply during harsh winters.

While polar bears and Arctic foxes are formidable predators in their own right, they coexist in the Arctic ecosystem, each playing a crucial role in maintaining the balance of nature. Polar bears, as top predators, help regulate the populations of seals and other prey species, while Arctic foxes contribute to the control of small rodent populations and aid in seed dispersal for Arctic plants.

Both polar bears and Arctic foxes are essential cultural symbols for indigenous Arctic communities. The Inuit and other indigenous peoples have deep spiritual connections with these animals, often incorporating them into their myths, legends, and traditional rituals.

The fate of polar bears and Arctic foxes is intrinsically linked to the health of the Arctic ecosystem. As climate change continues to reshape the region, the delicate balance of their habitats and food sources is disrupted. The loss of sea ice, changes in migratory patterns, and alterations in prey availability all pose challenges to their survival.

Conservation efforts and responsible management of Arctic resources are crucial in ensuring the continued existence of these apex predators. By protecting their habitats and addressing the impacts of climate change, we can safeguard the future of polar bears, Arctic foxes, and the entire Arctic ecosystem.

Arctic Birds: Migratory Wonders

In the vast expanse of the Arctic, the skies come alive with the extraordinary sight of migratory birds. These avian wonders embark on epic journeys, traveling thousands of miles to the Arctic each year in search of bountiful feeding grounds and safe havens for breeding.

One of the most remarkable migratory journeys in the avian world is undertaken by the Arctic tern (Sterna paradisaea). This small bird, weighing only a few ounces, travels astonishing distances from the Arctic to the Antarctic and back again. The Arctic tern's round-trip migration can span up to 44,000 miles annually, making it one of the longest migrations known among birds.

During the Arctic summer, the skies are graced by an array of seabirds that arrive to breed and raise their young. Puffins, guillemots, kittiwakes, fulmars, and other seabird species gather on the rocky cliffs and remote islands to establish nesting colonies. These seabirds are well-adapted to the Arctic's harsh conditions, using their sharp beaks to catch fish and other marine prey to nourish their chicks.

The common eider (Somateria mollissima) is another iconic Arctic bird, known for its striking appearance and valuable down feathers. Eiders are sea ducks that breed in the Arctic, building nests along the coasts and on islands. The female eider plucks down feathers from her breast to line her nest, providing excellent insulation for her eggs and chicks.

The Arctic's wetlands and tundra are also home to an abundance of migratory waterfowl. Ducks such as the northern pintail, the common teal, and the scaup undertake extensive migrations between their Arctic breeding grounds and warmer wintering areas further south. These waterfowl rely on the rich aquatic resources of the Arctic to feed and raise their young during the summer months.

The snowy owl (Bubo scandiacus) is a magnificent predator that thrives in the Arctic tundra. These owls have adapted to their frozen surroundings by sporting thick plumage and large talons, making them highly efficient hunters. Snowy owls are also migratory birds, and their movements are influenced by fluctuations in their primary prey, lemmings.

The red-throated loon (Gavia stellata) is a distinctive bird with a haunting, eerie call that resonates across Arctic lakes. During the breeding season, loons perform elaborate courtship displays, gracefully gliding across the water's surface in intricate patterns. These migratory birds spend their winters in coastal areas and open waters, where they feed on fish and crustaceans.

For many Arctic birds, the brief Arctic summer is a time of plenty and opportunity. The abundance of daylight and the explosion of insect life provide a feast for hungry chicks and adults alike. The challenge lies in taking full advantage of the short window of opportunity to feed, breed, and raise their young before the return migration journey begins.

Migration is not without its perils, and Arctic birds face a range of challenges during their journeys. Inclement weather, predation, and human interference pose threats to their survival. Climate change also affects migratory patterns, altering the availability of food and the timing of nesting and breeding activities.

Conservation efforts are crucial in protecting Arctic bird populations and their habitats. Many Arctic birds are designated as migratory species of international concern under various conservation agreements. Researchers and conservationists work tirelessly to monitor bird populations, study their behavior, and raise awareness about the importance of preserving Arctic habitats for these migratory wonders.

Arctic Wildlife Conservation: Protecting the Fragile Ecosystems

In the pristine and unforgiving landscapes of the Arctic, wildlife conservation takes on a whole new level of significance. The Arctic's fragile ecosystems support a rich tapestry of life, from iconic polar bears and graceful whales to elusive Arctic foxes and migratory birds. As human activities and climate change increasingly impact this delicate region, the need to protect Arctic wildlife and their habitats becomes more urgent than ever.

One of the most prominent Arctic conservation efforts centers around polar bears (Ursus maritimus). These majestic creatures, dependent on sea ice for hunting and breeding, face significant challenges due to climate change. As sea ice diminishes at an alarming rate, polar bears have to travel longer distances in search of food, leading to increased energy expenditure and decreased reproductive success.

The International Union for Conservation of Nature (IUCN) lists polar bears as vulnerable, and various international agreements aim to safeguard their survival. Organizations like the World Wildlife Fund (WWF) and Polar Bears International work tirelessly to study polar bear populations, monitor their habitats, and advocate for policies that mitigate climate change and protect critical Arctic habitats.

Marine mammals, such as whales and seals, are also the focus of intense conservation efforts. Whales, including belugas, narwhals, and bowhead whales, navigate the Arctic waters during their migrations. Overfishing, ship strikes, and ocean noise pollution threaten their well-being and disrupt their natural behaviors.

Seals, an essential prey for polar bears and other Arctic predators, are also subject to conservation efforts. The Marine Mammal Protection Act (MMPA) and other regional regulations aim to prevent the overexploitation of seals and protect their habitats. By safeguarding seal populations, we can maintain a balanced Arctic food web and support the livelihoods of indigenous communities that rely on seals for food and cultural practices.

Birds, particularly migratory species, play a vital role in Arctic ecosystems and beyond. Many Arctic birds, like the Arctic tern and the red-throated loon, undertake extraordinary migrations between the Arctic and other regions. The protection of their nesting sites and wintering areas is crucial in ensuring their survival. Climate change poses a significant threat to Arctic wildlife, with rising temperatures altering migration patterns, breeding times, and food availability. Arctic habitats are undergoing rapid changes, affecting the distribution and behavior of many species. Conserving these fragile ecosystems requires collective efforts to reduce greenhouse gas emissions, support renewable energy sources, and promote sustainable practices worldwide.

Indigenous peoples have long been stewards of the Arctic's natural resources and have invaluable knowledge of the land and its wildlife. Collaborating with indigenous communities in conservation initiatives is essential in creating effective and culturally sensitive strategies. The Arctic Council, an international forum comprising Arctic countries and indigenous representatives, plays a crucial role in addressing environmental challenges in the Arctic. The Council focuses on issues like climate change, conservation, and sustainable development, bringing together scientific research and local knowledge to inform policy decisions.

Protected areas, such as national parks and wildlife reserves, serve as sanctuaries for Arctic wildlife. These designated zones offer refuge from human disturbance and provide essential habitats for breeding, nesting, and feeding. Strict regulations govern activities within these areas to minimize human impact on wildlife and their environments. Educational programs and ecotourism initiatives also play a part in Arctic conservation efforts. By fostering an understanding of the Arctic's unique biodiversity and promoting responsible tourism practices, we can inspire people to become advocates for Arctic wildlife and ecosystems.

Conserving Arctic wildlife is not just about preserving individual species but safeguarding the entire ecosystem and the vital services it provides to the planet. Arctic ecosystems contribute to global climate regulation, carbon sequestration, and ocean circulation, making their protection critical for the health of the entire planet.

Arctic Ocean Exploration: Unraveling the Abyss

The Arctic Ocean, with its icy expanse and remote depths, has long captured the curiosity of explorers and scientists alike. The quest to unravel the mysteries of this vast and enigmatic ocean has led to some of the most remarkable and groundbreaking expeditions in human history.

Early Arctic explorers, driven by the allure of uncharted territories and the search for new trade routes, braved treacherous conditions to reach the North Pole and explore the Arctic Ocean. One of the most famous expeditions was that of Roald Amundsen, who led the first successful journey to the North Pole in 1926. His expedition provided valuable insights into the Arctic's geography and ice conditions.

As technology advanced, so did Arctic exploration. Submarines allowed scientists to venture into the ocean's depths, revealing a world beneath the ice that was previously unknown. These submarines provided vital data on water temperatures, salinity, and marine life, contributing to our understanding of the Arctic's complex ecosystem.

The Arctic Ocean is unique in that it is almost completely surrounded by land, making it a semi-enclosed basin. It is the smallest and shallowest of the world's five oceans, covering an area of about 5.4 million square miles and reaching an average depth of approximately 3,240 feet. The ocean's deepest point, known as the Eurasian Basin Deep, plunges to a staggering 17,881 feet.

One of the most significant challenges in Arctic oceanography is the presence of sea ice. The Arctic's ice cover fluctuates with the seasons, reaching its maximum extent during the winter and shrinking significantly during the summer. This dynamic ice cover influences the ocean's circulation patterns, marine ecosystems, and the Earth's climate system.

The Arctic Ocean is home to a diverse array of marine life, from microscopic organisms to large mammals. Polar bears, walruses, and seals are among the most iconic inhabitants of the Arctic's icy waters. The polar bear, in particular, relies on sea ice for hunting and resting, making it one of the most vulnerable species to the impacts of climate change.

The Arctic Ocean also serves as a vital breeding and feeding ground for numerous bird species, such as the Arctic tern and the common eider. These migratory birds travel vast distances to reach the Arctic, taking advantage of the rich feeding opportunities during the short Arctic summer.

In recent years, climate change has had a profound impact on the Arctic Ocean. Rising temperatures have led to a rapid decline in sea ice extent and thickness, affecting the Arctic's ecosystems and the communities that rely on ice for transportation and subsistence hunting.

Arctic oceanography plays a crucial role in monitoring and understanding these changes. Researchers use a variety of tools, such as satellites, underwater robots, and buoys, to collect data on sea ice extent, water temperature, and salinity. These data provide essential insights into the dynamics of the Arctic Ocean and its response to climate change.

The Arctic is also a hotbed for scientific research related to climate change. Scientists study the region's past climate through ice cores, which offer a record of ancient atmospheric conditions and greenhouse gas concentrations. This information helps in predicting future climate scenarios and understanding the global implications of Arctic warming.

The Arctic Ocean is not only a frontier for scientific exploration but also a potential area of economic interest. As the ice recedes, there is growing interest in accessing the region's vast reserves of oil, gas, and minerals. However, the delicate Arctic ecosystem and its vulnerable wildlife underscore the need for responsible and sustainable development.

International cooperation is essential in Arctic exploration and conservation efforts. The Arctic Council, consisting of Arctic nations and indigenous representatives, facilitates dialogue and cooperation on matters relating to the Arctic environment and sustainable development.

Mysteries of the Aurora Borealis: Northern Lights Revealed

In the far reaches of the Arctic skies, a breathtaking and ethereal spectacle unfolds – the Aurora Borealis, also known as the Northern Lights. This mesmerizing light display has captivated humans for centuries, inspiring myths, legends, and scientific inquiry. As we gaze upon this celestial wonder, we are drawn into the mysteries of the Aurora Borealis, seeking to understand the science and magic behind its radiant dance.

The Aurora Borealis is a natural light display that occurs predominantly in high-latitude regions near the Earth's magnetic poles. In the Arctic, it is known as the Aurora Borealis, while in the Antarctic, it is called the Aurora Australis. Both phenomena are caused by interactions between solar particles and the Earth's magnetic field.

The source of the Aurora Borealis lies over 93 million miles away – the Sun. It all begins with solar flares and coronal mass ejections, releasing charged particles, mainly electrons and protons, into space. When these solar particles reach the Earth, they collide with the gases in our atmosphere, such as nitrogen and oxygen.

As the solar particles interact with the atmospheric gases, they transfer energy to the gas molecules, exciting them to higher energy levels. When these excited molecules return to their original state, they release the excess energy in the form of light, creating the vibrant colors of the Aurora Borealis.

The most common color of the Northern Lights is green, produced when solar particles collide with oxygen at lower altitudes. Occasionally, the Aurora can display red, purple, blue, and even pink hues, depending on the altitude and the type of gas involved in the collision.

The shape and movement of the Aurora Borealis add to its mystique. The lights can appear as swirling curtains, arches, or pulsating waves across the sky. These dynamic patterns are influenced by the Earth's magnetic field and the solar wind's variations, which can change from minute to minute.

The best time to witness the Aurora Borealis is during the winter months, from September to April, when the Arctic nights are at their longest and the skies are darkest. The best viewing locations are far away from light pollution, where the Northern Lights can paint the sky with their celestial brushstrokes.

Indigenous cultures in the Arctic have rich folklore and legends surrounding the Aurora Borealis. Some believe the lights to be the spirits of their ancestors or mythical creatures playing in the sky. The Inuit people of Canada and Alaska tell stories of the Aurora being the spirits of animals they hunted.

Scientific understanding of the Aurora Borealis has advanced significantly over the years. Ground-based observatories and satellites have allowed researchers to study the phenomenon in detail. The study of the Aurora Borealis falls under the field of space physics, a branch of science that explores the interactions between the Sun, Earth, and the space environment.

One of the most intriguing aspects of the Northern Lights is their cyclic nature. The intensity and frequency of the Aurora are tied to the solar activity cycle, which follows an 11-year pattern of solar flares and sunspots. During periods of high solar activity, the Aurora Borealis becomes more frequent and intense, delighting skywatchers with more vivid displays.

Tourism revolving around the Aurora Borealis has boomed in recent years, with travelers from around the world seeking to witness this celestial phenomenon in all its glory. Destinations like Norway, Sweden, Iceland, Canada, and Alaska have become popular Aurora-watching spots, offering unforgettable experiences under the dancing lights.

Chasing Ice: Climate Change in the Arctic

In the vast and frozen wilderness of the Arctic, a profound transformation is underway. Climate change, fueled by human activities and the burning of fossil fuels, is reshaping the Arctic landscape at an alarming rate. As the Earth's temperatures rise, the Arctic is warming twice as fast as the global average, ushering in a new era of environmental challenges and consequences.

One of the most striking indicators of Arctic climate change is the rapid decline of sea ice. The Arctic sea ice cover, which has been a defining feature of the region for thousands of years, is diminishing both in extent and thickness. Satellite observations and scientific studies have shown that the summer sea ice extent has decreased by about 13% per decade since the late 1970s.

The loss of sea ice has far-reaching implications for the Arctic ecosystem and the communities that depend on ice for their livelihoods. Polar bears, whose hunting and breeding behaviors are intricately tied to sea ice, face increasing challenges in finding food and suitable habitats. The melting of sea ice also affects other marine species, including seals and walruses, that rely on the ice as platforms for resting and giving birth.

The Arctic's melting ice also contributes to rising sea levels globally. As ice from glaciers and ice sheets in Greenland and Antarctica melts, it adds water to the oceans, causing coastlines to erode and low-lying areas to become more vulnerable to flooding. Coastal communities in the Arctic and around the world are facing the reality of climate-induced displacement and loss of cultural heritage.

The Arctic permafrost, the layer of frozen soil that underlies much of the region, is also thawing due to rising temperatures. Permafrost contains vast amounts of organic carbon, which has been preserved in frozen state for millennia. As permafrost thaws, this carbon is released into the atmosphere as carbon dioxide and methane, potent greenhouse gases that further exacerbate global warming.

The thawing permafrost also poses infrastructure challenges, as buildings, roads, and pipelines built on frozen ground become unstable. Indigenous communities, in particular, are grappling with the impacts of permafrost thaw, as traditional ways of life and subsistence practices are disrupted.

The melting Arctic is not just a regional issue; it has global ramifications. The Arctic acts as a climate regulator, influencing weather patterns and ocean currents around the world. Changes in the Arctic can affect the jet stream, which plays a crucial role in determining weather patterns in the mid-latitudes. Alterations in ocean circulation, driven by Arctic warming, can also impact weather and climate far beyond the polar region.

The Paris Agreement, adopted in 2015, brought together nations to combat climate change and limit global warming to well below 2 degrees Celsius above pre-industrial levels. The agreement recognizes the special vulnerability of the Arctic and the need for urgent action to address its unique challenges.

Arctic nations and the international community are taking steps to address climate change in the region. Efforts to reduce greenhouse gas emissions, transition to renewable energy sources, and support sustainable practices are gaining momentum. Collaborative research and monitoring initiatives are also helping to advance our understanding of Arctic climate change and inform policy decisions.

The Arctic Council, composed of Arctic nations and indigenous representatives, serves as a platform for dialogue and cooperation on Arctic environmental issues. The council addresses topics like climate change, pollution, and biodiversity conservation, fostering international collaboration in the face of shared challenges.

Chasing ice and understanding the consequences of climate change in the Arctic is a critical mission for scientists, environmentalists, and policymakers. By studying the impacts of climate change in the Arctic, we gain valuable insights into the complex interplay between human activities and the natural environment.

The challenges posed by climate change in the Arctic are immense, but they also present an opportunity for collective action and change. By embracing renewable energy, promoting sustainable practices, and prioritizing environmental conservation, we can safeguard the Arctic and our planet for future generations.

Indigenous Art and Crafts: Expressing Arctic Spirituality

In the vast and frozen landscapes of the Arctic, the indigenous peoples have thrived for millennia, preserving their cultures and traditions through art and crafts. From intricately carved sculptures to vibrant textiles and delicate beadwork, indigenous art in the Arctic is a profound expression of spirituality, history, and connection to the land.

Art has been an integral part of indigenous cultures in the Arctic for generations. It is not merely a form of creative expression but also a way to convey stories, myths, and beliefs that are passed down from one generation to the next. Through their art, indigenous people honor their ancestors, celebrate their spiritual beliefs, and demonstrate their intimate relationship with the natural world.

One of the most iconic forms of indigenous art in the Arctic is Inuit carving. Inuit artists, known for their exceptional skill in working with stone, bone, and ivory, create intricate sculptures that depict animals, spirits, and scenes from everyday life. Each carving is imbued with symbolism and meaning, reflecting the spiritual beliefs and cultural heritage of the Inuit people.

Inuit art also includes prints and drawings, often showcasing themes of hunting, family, and the surrounding landscapes. The art of printmaking, introduced to the Arctic in the 1950s, has become a powerful medium for Inuit artists to share their stories with the world.

In Alaska and northern Canada, the indigenous peoples of the Northwest Coast are renowned for their stunning totem poles and wooden masks. These works of art are intricately carved from red cedar and adorned with symbols representing family crests, spirits, and ancestral stories. Totem poles, in particular, are erected as monumental expressions of spiritual and cultural significance, often serving as markers for tribal territories or commemorating important events.

The art of beadwork is also prevalent among indigenous communities in the Arctic. Traditionally, beads were made from materials like ivory, bone, and shells, but today, they are often sourced from trade or commerce. Beadwork is used to decorate clothing, accessories, and ceremonial regalia, and each design carries special meanings and connections to the natural world.

Indigenous art in the Arctic is deeply intertwined with spirituality and ceremonies. Masks, for instance, play a crucial role in traditional dances and rituals, allowing individuals to embody spiritual beings and ancestors. These performances are essential for passing down cultural knowledge and maintaining spiritual connections.

In recent years, indigenous art from the Arctic has gained global recognition and appreciation. Art galleries and museums around the world showcase the works of indigenous artists, providing a platform for their voices to be heard and their cultures to be celebrated.

The creation and sale of indigenous art have also become an important economic activity for Arctic communities. It provides an avenue for artists to support their families and preserve their cultural heritage while sharing their unique perspectives and stories with a wider audience.

However, as the demand for indigenous art grows, there is a need to ensure that artists' rights and cultural heritage are protected. Issues of cultural appropriation and fair compensation for artists have sparked discussions about the responsible collection and distribution of indigenous art.

Efforts to promote and preserve indigenous art and crafts in the Arctic are ongoing. Organizations like the Inuit Art Foundation and the Arctic Indigenous Arts Initiative support indigenous artists by providing resources, education, and opportunities to showcase their work.

Indigenous art in the Arctic continues to evolve as new generations of artists embrace traditional techniques while also exploring contemporary forms of expression. Through their art, indigenous people in the Arctic remain steadfast in preserving their spiritual connections, cultural identities, and profound reverence for the land and its creatures.

Arctic Music and Dance: Rhythms of the North

In the frigid and enchanting Arctic, music and dance echo the soul of its indigenous peoples, weaving tales of their rich cultural heritage and deep spiritual connection to the land. From the haunting melodies of throat singing to the rhythmic beats of drum dances, the Arctic's music and dance traditions are a vibrant tapestry of artistic expression.

Inuit throat singing, also known as katajjaq, is a mesmerizing vocal tradition that has been practiced for centuries among Inuit women. This ancient art form involves two women facing each other, engaging in a friendly yet competitive vocal duet. Through a series of rhythmic inhalations and exhalations, the singers create intricate and harmonic sounds that mimic the natural world, such as the wind, animals, and water. Katajjaq is not only a form of entertainment but also a way for Inuit women to bond and communicate non-verbally.

Another captivating musical tradition of the Arctic is the drum dance, found among the indigenous peoples of Alaska, Canada, and Greenland. These drum dances are communal events that bring together the community for celebrations, ceremonies, and storytelling. The beat of the drum and the movement of the dancers are intimately connected to the rhythms of the Arctic landscape and the spirits that inhabit it.

The Inupiat people of Alaska, for example, have the blanket toss dance, where dancers are propelled into the air on a walrus skin blanket, symbolizing the relationship between humans and the animals they depend on for survival. In Canada, the Inuit have the drum dance, where songs are sung in praise of nature, animals, and ancestral spirits, and the drumbeat connects the dancers to the heartbeat of the Earth.

Drums, a central element in Arctic music, are often made from materials like sealskin, caribou hide, or even driftwood, each with its unique sound. The drums are beautifully decorated with intricate designs and patterns, often reflecting the natural world and spiritual beliefs of the indigenous people.

Arctic music and dance are not just isolated performances; they are deeply embedded in the fabric of everyday life and cultural identity. Indigenous communities in the Arctic have a wealth of songs that recount their history, legends, and ancestral wisdom. Through these musical traditions, knowledge is passed down from one generation to the next, preserving the collective memory of the people.

The rhythms of Arctic music and dance vary across regions and communities, each reflecting the distinct cultural nuances of the indigenous groups. The Yupik people of Alaska, for instance, have yuraq, a dance that combines graceful movements with the rhythmic sounds of the drum and hand clapping. In Greenland, the Inuit have the drum dance called "avivaq," where dancers mimic the movements of animals and birds.

In addition to traditional music and dance, contemporary Arctic artists are also exploring innovative ways to merge ancient traditions with modern influences. Music festivals, such as the Arctic Sounds Festival in Greenland and the Alianait Arts Festival in Canada, celebrate the diversity of Arctic music and provide platforms for emerging artists to share their unique voices with the world.

The Arctic's music and dance are not only a source of cultural pride but also a means of promoting intercultural exchange. In recent years, collaborations between Arctic artists and musicians from other parts of the world have resulted in captivating fusions of styles and sounds, bringing the spirit of the North to global audiences.

As we immerse ourselves in the rhythms of the Arctic, we are transported to a world of vibrant colors, untamed wilderness, and the enduring spirit of its people. The music and dance of the Arctic are more than artistic expressions; they are a celebration of life, resilience, and the profound connections between humanity and the natural world.

By embracing and appreciating Arctic music and dance, we honor the artistic legacy of the indigenous peoples and affirm the importance of preserving their cultural heritage. As we move to the rhythms of the North, we become part of a timeless narrative that speaks of the human spirit's capacity to find joy, beauty, and meaning even in the harshest and most remote corners of the Earth.

Arctic Traditions: From Storytelling to Shamanism

In the vast and enchanting Arctic, traditions run deep, carrying the wisdom and spirituality of its indigenous peoples through generations. These traditions are more than mere customs; they are the threads that weave together the cultural tapestry of the Arctic.

Storytelling is at the heart of Arctic traditions. For thousands of years, indigenous elders have passed down myths, legends, and ancestral knowledge through oral narratives. These stories, often filled with magical creatures, heroic deeds, and lessons for life, serve not only as entertainment but also as a way to preserve cultural identity and pass on invaluable wisdom.

The oral traditions of the Arctic have helped shape the beliefs and values of indigenous communities. They provide a profound connection to the land, animals, and spirits that inhabit the frozen wilderness. The stories often carry moral lessons, teaching respect for nature and the interconnectedness of all living beings.

Inuit mythology, for example, is rich with stories of powerful beings like Sedna, the sea goddess, and Nanook, the polar bear spirit. These stories explain the origins of the world, the changing seasons, and the cycle of life and death. They also emphasize the importance of harmony with nature and the spirits that govern the Arctic landscape.

Another essential aspect of Arctic traditions is shamanism, a spiritual practice that has been integral to indigenous cultures for thousands of years. Shamans, known as angakkuqs among the Inuit and noaidis among the Sámi, serve as intermediaries between the human and spirit worlds.

Shamanism involves rituals, ceremonies, and trance-like states to communicate with spirits, seek guidance, and heal the sick. Shamans are believed to possess supernatural powers and are highly respected members of their communities. They play a vital role in maintaining balance and harmony in the Arctic's delicate ecosystem.

Shamans also serve as storytellers and keepers of cultural knowledge. Through their visions and dreams, they gain insight into the spiritual world and communicate with ancestors and spirits. Their stories, like the ancient myths, help shape the cultural identity and beliefs of the Arctic's indigenous peoples. Arctic traditions also include various forms of celebration and ritual. Festivals and ceremonies are essential events that mark significant milestones in life, such as births, coming-of-age, and marriages. These gatherings bring communities together, fostering a sense of unity and connection with each other and the natural world.

Ceremonial practices often involve music, dance, and art. Drum dances, mask performances, and throat singing are all integral to the spiritual and communal aspects of Arctic traditions. These rituals reinforce the interdependence between humans and the environment and strengthen the bonds among community members. The relationship between indigenous peoples and the Arctic environment is deeply spiritual. Land, water, and animals are considered sacred, and the customs and rituals are closely tied to the natural cycles and rhythms of life. The Arctic's harsh and unpredictable climate has shaped these traditions, teaching respect for nature's forces and the need for adaptation and resilience.

Despite the challenges posed by modernization and globalization, Arctic traditions continue to thrive. Indigenous communities are actively working to preserve and revitalize their cultural heritage. Initiatives such as language revitalization, cultural education programs, and traditional art workshops are helping to keep these ancient practices alive. Arctic traditions are not static; they evolve and adapt to the changing times while maintaining their essence. The resilience of these traditions is a testament to the enduring spirit of the Arctic's indigenous peoples and their commitment to preserving their cultural identity for future generations.

By understanding and appreciating Arctic traditions, we gain insight into the wisdom and resilience of the Arctic's indigenous communities. Their stories, ceremonies, and spiritual practices offer valuable lessons on living in harmony with nature, respecting diverse cultures, and embracing the power of storytelling to connect us to our shared human heritage.

Thule Culture: Ancient Arctic Societies

In the frozen expanse of the Arctic, long before the arrival of European explorers, a remarkable culture thrived - the Thule culture. The Thule people were the ancestors of modern-day Inuit and Yupik communities, and their history is a testament to the resilience and adaptability of human societies in extreme environments.

The Thule culture emerged around 1000 CE and lasted until the early 20th century. They were nomadic hunter-gatherers, adept at navigating the harsh Arctic landscape and utilizing its resources for survival. The Thule people were skilled hunters, relying on the rich marine life, such as seals, whales, and fish, for sustenance and materials for their tools and clothing.

One of the most iconic features of Thule culture is their ingenious invention - the kayak. These slender, lightweight boats were expertly crafted from driftwood or whalebone and covered in sealskin. Kayaks enabled the Thule people to travel vast distances across the Arctic waters, expanding their territories and facilitating trade and cultural exchange between different communities.

The Thule culture was highly adaptable, and as they migrated across the Arctic, they encountered and absorbed various elements from other cultures they encountered. This adaptability allowed them to integrate new technologies and knowledge into their own practices, enhancing their capacity to thrive in their challenging environment.

In addition to their exceptional hunting and navigational skills, the Thule people were skilled artisans. They created intricate carvings, sculptures, and tools from bone, ivory, and antler, showcasing their artistic talents and deep spiritual connections with the natural world.

As the Thule people traversed the Arctic, they established semi-permanent settlements and developed social structures. Their communities were often centered around communal dwellings, known as qargi or kashim, which served as meeting places for ceremonies, social gatherings, and decision-making.

Family and community were central to Thule society. The extended family, known as the kinship group, formed the basis of their social organization. These kinship groups provided essential support and cooperation for survival, as the Arctic required collective effort to overcome its challenges.

Spirituality was deeply ingrained in Thule culture. They held a profound belief in the interconnectedness of all living beings and the spiritual significance of the animals they relied on for survival. Shamans played a vital role in their spiritual practices, communicating with spirits and ancestors through rituals and ceremonies.

In the early 20th century, the Thule culture underwent a significant transition with the arrival of European explorers and traders. While some aspects of traditional Thule culture persisted, the influx of foreign influences brought about changes in their lifestyles, technologies, and trade patterns.

Today, the legacy of the Thule culture lives on in the customs, traditions, and languages of modern-day Inuit and Yupik communities. Their knowledge of survival in the Arctic, their mastery of hunting and navigation, and their rich artistic traditions continue to shape the identity and resilience of indigenous Arctic societies.

Archaeological research and ongoing connections with indigenous communities provide valuable insights into the ancient Thule culture. The study of Thule artifacts and the stories passed down through generations contribute to our understanding of the complexities and diversity of human history in the Arctic.

The Thule culture serves as a reminder of the remarkable adaptability and ingenuity of human societies, as well as the enduring connections between culture, environment, and spirituality. As we learn from the ancient wisdom of the Thule people, we are inspired to embrace resilience, honor our interconnectedness with nature, and celebrate the diversity of human cultures that have thrived in the Arctic's frozen embrace.

Arctic Architecture: Building in Extreme Environments

In the vast and unforgiving landscapes of the Arctic, architecture takes on a unique and formidable challenge - to create structures that can withstand the harshest of climates. From traditional igloos to modern sustainable designs, Arctic architecture reflects the ingenuity and resourcefulness of human beings in adapting to extreme environments.

The traditional dwelling of the Arctic, the igloo, is a symbol of human resilience in the face of adversity. Constructed from blocks of compacted snow, the igloo's dome-shaped design maximizes interior space and minimizes heat loss. The insulating properties of the snow keep the interior surprisingly warm, providing a refuge from the biting cold outside.

While igloos are no longer the primary form of housing in the Arctic, they remain an essential part of cultural heritage, a testament to the intimate relationship between indigenous peoples and their environment. In some remote regions, modern adaptations of the igloo are still used for temporary shelters during hunting and travel.

Modern Arctic architecture combines traditional wisdom with innovative technologies. Architects and engineers have developed sustainable and energy-efficient designs to meet the unique challenges of the Arctic climate. These buildings incorporate advanced insulation, solar panels, and efficient heating systems to reduce energy consumption and environmental impact.

One prevalent form of modern Arctic architecture is the "passive house" concept. These structures are carefully designed to retain heat during the long and frigid winters while keeping cool during the short summer months. Passive houses use thick insulation, airtight windows, and mechanical ventilation systems to maintain a comfortable indoor environment without excessive energy consumption.

Arctic architecture is not limited to residential buildings. In remote communities, where access to resources is limited, public buildings like schools, community centers, and medical facilities play a crucial role in fostering social cohesion and providing essential services.

To build these structures, architects and construction teams often face logistical challenges. Extreme weather, remote locations, and limited resources demand careful planning and creative problem-solving. Materials must be transported over vast distances, and construction often occurs during brief warm periods.

In some Arctic communities, buildings are constructed on stilts or pilings to prevent them from sinking into the permafrost as temperatures fluctuate. These innovative techniques allow buildings to remain stable and functional despite the shifting ground below. As climate change impacts the Arctic, architects are also focusing on designing buildings that are resilient to its effects. Rising temperatures and thawing permafrost pose new challenges to infrastructure stability. Engineers are exploring innovative foundation designs and materials to mitigate the impacts of these changes.

Arctic architecture is not just about functionality; it also celebrates cultural identity and reflects the values of the communities it serves. Inuit and Sámi communities, for instance, incorporate traditional design elements and indigenous artwork into modern buildings, connecting contemporary structures to their rich cultural heritage. In recent years, sustainable and ecologically friendly design principles have gained prominence in Arctic architecture. There is a growing recognition of the importance of respecting and preserving the fragile Arctic ecosystem in the construction and operation of buildings.

Efforts to engage local communities in the design and construction process are also becoming more common. Collaborating with indigenous peoples ensures that buildings are culturally appropriate, meet the needs of the community, and respect traditional knowledge and practices.

Arctic architecture is an evolving and dynamic field that continues to adapt to the challenges of the changing Arctic environment. It is a testament to the human capacity for innovation, adaptation, and respect for the delicate balance between human settlements and the natural world.

Languages of the North: From Inuktitut to Sami

In the vast and diverse expanse of the Arctic, a rich tapestry of languages reflects the cultural heritage and ancient wisdom of the indigenous peoples. From the intricate phonetics of Inuktitut to the melodious cadences of Sami, the languages of the North are a living testament to the resilience and complexity of human communication.

One of the most widely spoken languages in the Arctic is Inuktitut. It is the language of the Inuit people, who inhabit regions across Canada, Greenland, and Alaska. Inuktitut is known for its polysynthetic nature, allowing for the creation of long and descriptive words that convey detailed meanings in a single word. This linguistic feature is particularly useful in describing the nuances of the Arctic landscape, its animals, and the rich cultural traditions of the Inuit.

The Sami people, who inhabit the northern regions of Scandinavia, speak a diverse group of languages known as Sami languages. These languages are part of the Uralic language family, which includes Finnish and Estonian. Sami languages vary significantly between different regions and communities, with each having its unique set of phonetics, grammar, and vocabulary.

Another important language of the Arctic is Greenlandic, spoken primarily in Greenland. Greenlandic is an Eskimo-Aleut language closely related to Inuktitut. Like Inuktitut, Greenlandic is characterized by its complex word structure, enabling speakers to communicate intricate concepts in concise forms.

Throughout the Arctic, indigenous communities maintain a strong connection to their ancestral languages. These languages are not just a means of communication but also a vital aspect of cultural identity and heritage. They carry the stories, myths, and traditional knowledge of the indigenous peoples, connecting them to their ancestors and the land they have inhabited for thousands of years.

However, like many indigenous languages worldwide, Arctic languages face challenges. The influence of dominant languages, such as English and Russian, has led to a decrease in the number of fluent speakers among younger generations. Efforts to preserve and revitalize these languages are ongoing, with language immersion programs, language revitalization initiatives, and documentation of oral histories being vital steps in maintaining linguistic diversity.

Linguists and scholars recognize the importance of preserving these endangered languages, not only for the indigenous communities but also for humanity as a whole. Arctic languages hold unique insights into the environment, cultural practices, and belief systems of their speakers, contributing to a broader understanding of human diversity and the intricate relationship between language and culture.

In recent years, there has been an increased focus on supporting language revitalization efforts and promoting multilingualism in Arctic communities. Educational programs that incorporate indigenous languages into the curriculum are crucial in nurturing a new generation of fluent speakers and fostering a sense of pride in cultural identity.

The languages of the North are not just tools for communication but also vessels of cultural wisdom and resilience. As we celebrate and preserve these unique linguistic heritages, we honor the enduring spirit and cultural richness of the Arctic's indigenous peoples. Their languages are bridges that connect the past with the present and pave the way for future generations to embrace their heritage and carry it forward into the ever-changing Arctic landscape.

Arctic Transportation: Navigating the Frozen Waters

In the vast and icy expanse of the Arctic, transportation has always been a formidable challenge. From ancient times to modern innovations, the people of the North have developed ingenious methods to navigate the frozen waters and connect communities across the region.

Historically, one of the primary modes of transportation in the Arctic was by boat. Indigenous peoples crafted boats from materials such as sealskin, driftwood, or whalebone. These lightweight and flexible boats were ideal for navigating the treacherous Arctic waters, allowing for swift travel between coastal settlements and hunting grounds.

Kayaks, a remarkable invention of the Arctic, were essential for hunting and exploration. These slender, one-person boats were crafted with remarkable precision and ingenuity. Their design enabled hunters to stealthily approach marine animals, such as seals and whales, for sustenance and materials. Kayaking remains an integral part of Arctic culture today, with traditional kayaking events and races celebrated in some communities.

In the modern era, technology and innovation have transformed Arctic transportation. Ships and icebreakers equipped with advanced navigation systems now traverse the Arctic's frozen waters, facilitating trade, scientific exploration, and tourism. These vessels are crucial for supplying remote communities, delivering goods, and providing essential services to the region.

The Northern Sea Route, also known as the Northeast Passage, has gained significance as ice recedes due to climate change. This maritime route connects Europe and Asia via the Arctic Ocean, significantly reducing the distance and time required for shipping between these continents. The opening of the Northern Sea Route has the potential to reshape global trade patterns and presents both opportunities and challenges for Arctic communities and the environment.

The Northwest Passage is another historically significant route through the Arctic waters. This passage, which traverses Canada's

Arctic Archipelago, was sought after by explorers for centuries as a shorter route from Europe to Asia. However, the Northwest Passage remained largely impassable due to thick ice and treacherous conditions. Today, with changing ice conditions, the passage is increasingly navigable, though it still presents significant challenges for shipping and navigation.

Air travel is also essential for connecting Arctic communities, especially in remote areas where road and water transportation are limited. Small aircraft and helicopters provide vital lifelines for delivering medical supplies, conducting scientific research, and supporting search and rescue operations.

One of the most daring and iconic forms of transportation in the Arctic is the dog sled. For thousands of years, indigenous peoples have used dog sleds as a means of transportation, hunting, and exploration. Sled dogs, such as the Siberian Husky and the Alaskan Malamute, are highly adapted to the Arctic environment, with thick fur and powerful stamina to endure long journeys in freezing temperatures.

While traditional dog sleds continue to be used by some communities, modern snowmobiles have become prevalent for transportation and recreation across the Arctic. Snowmobiles provide faster travel over snow and ice, enabling access to more remote regions and facilitating economic activities like hunting and tourism.

Despite the advancements in transportation, the Arctic remains a challenging environment to navigate, especially during the winter months when ice and extreme cold present significant obstacles. Transporting goods and resources requires careful planning and coordination, considering weather conditions and seasonal changes.

The future of Arctic transportation is influenced by the impacts of climate change. As the Arctic continues to warm, the melting ice may create new opportunities for shipping and resource extraction. However, it also poses risks to the delicate Arctic ecosystem and the livelihoods of indigenous communities that depend on the region's natural resources.

The Northern Sea Route: Shipping in the Arctic

The Northern Sea Route, also known as the Northeast Passage, is a maritime route that traverses the Arctic Ocean, connecting the Atlantic and Pacific Oceans along the northern coast of Russia. This historic and strategic route has captured the attention of explorers, traders, and policymakers for centuries. Today, as climate change leads to the melting of Arctic ice, the Northern Sea Route is gaining renewed significance as a potential shortcut for global shipping and trade.

The allure of the Northern Sea Route lies in its potential to reduce shipping times and costs. Traditionally, ships traveling between Europe and Asia have had to take the longer route through the Suez Canal or around the southern tip of Africa, adding considerable time and expense to their journey. By navigating the Northern Sea Route, vessels can significantly shorten their transit time, making it an attractive alternative for certain types of cargo.

The Northern Sea Route stretches from the Bering Strait in the east to the Kara Sea in the west, covering approximately 5,600 kilometers (3,480 miles). It passes through several bodies of water, including the Chukchi Sea, East Siberian Sea, Laptev Sea, and the Kara Sea, before reaching the Barents Sea near the Norwegian coast.

Despite its potential advantages, the Northern Sea Route poses significant challenges for shipping. The Arctic's harsh and unpredictable weather, coupled with the presence of ice, makes navigation hazardous and requires careful planning. The route is only open for a short period during the summer months when ice levels are at their lowest, making it a seasonal passage.

Icebreakers play a crucial role in ensuring safe navigation along the Northern Sea Route. These specialized vessels are designed to break through thick ice, creating a path for other ships to follow. Russia, being the primary country bordering the Northern Sea Route, has a fleet of icebreakers that assist in escorting ships and maintaining ice-free channels during the navigation season.

As the Arctic continues to warm at a faster rate than other regions, the extent and thickness of sea ice have been decreasing. This trend has led to longer ice-free periods along the Northern Sea Route, increasing the window of opportunity for shipping. Some studies suggest that the Northern Sea Route could be navigable for up to six months in the future if current climate trends persist.

The decreasing ice cover and longer navigable periods have prompted interest from various stakeholders, including shipping companies, resource industries, and governments. Several countries, including Russia, China, and European nations, have expressed growing interest in the potential economic and geopolitical advantages of the route.

However, the increased use of the Northern Sea Route also raises concerns about its environmental impact. The Arctic is a delicate ecosystem, home to unique and vulnerable species, including polar bears, seals, and various seabirds. Increased shipping traffic can lead to the risk of oil spills, ship strikes, and noise pollution, all of which can have detrimental effects on the region's biodiversity.

Moreover, the melting Arctic ice and the opening of new shipping routes have raised questions about sovereignty and territorial claims. As the region becomes more accessible, there has been growing competition among nations to assert their influence and control over the Arctic's resources and sea routes.

International cooperation and responsible governance are essential for ensuring the sustainable and safe use of the Northern Sea Route. The Arctic Council, an intergovernmental forum that includes Arctic countries and indigenous representatives, plays a crucial role in addressing issues related to the Arctic, including shipping regulations, environmental protection, and indigenous rights.

Arctic Policy and Governance: Balancing Interests

The Arctic, with its vast expanse of frozen landscapes and abundant natural resources, has become a focal point of interest for nations and stakeholders around the world. As the region's ice continues to melt due to climate change, opportunities for resource extraction, shipping, and scientific research have multiplied. With these opportunities come challenges in balancing the diverse interests and concerns of various stakeholders.

The Arctic is home to eight countries: Canada, Denmark (through Greenland), Finland, Iceland, Norway, Russia, Sweden, and the United States (through Alaska). Each of these nations has different political systems, laws, and policies, which can complicate matters when addressing Arctic governance and resource management.

The Arctic Council, established in 1996, is a key international forum for cooperation and decision-making in the Arctic region. It consists of the eight Arctic states and representatives of indigenous peoples in the region. The Arctic Council focuses on issues related to environmental protection, sustainable development, and scientific research. It promotes dialogue and collaboration among member countries, ensuring that decisions take into account the unique needs and perspectives of indigenous communities. One of the primary challenges facing Arctic governance is striking a balance between economic development and environmental protection. The region's natural resources, including oil, gas, minerals, and fisheries, are highly valuable commodities. However, their extraction and exploitation can have significant environmental impacts, threatening the fragile Arctic ecosystem and its biodiversity.

Environmental concerns in the Arctic are further compounded by the effects of climate change, which are more pronounced in this region than in most other parts of the world. The melting ice and rising sea levels not only impact the Arctic's unique wildlife but also pose risks to coastal communities and infrastructures. Developing policies that address climate change and promote sustainable practices are crucial for the long-term health of the region. Indigenous peoples in the Arctic play a vital role in Arctic governance. They have lived in harmony with the environment for thousands of years and possess valuable traditional knowledge of the land, wildlife, and climate. Recognizing and respecting the rights of indigenous peoples, including their land rights and self-determination, is fundamental to achieving balanced and effective Arctic policies. In addition to the Arctic Council, other international organizations and treaties play a role in Arctic governance. For example, the United Nations Convention on the Law of the Sea (UNCLOS) provides a framework for the delimitation of maritime boundaries and the allocation of rights and responsibilities in the Arctic's waters. UNCLOS ensures that disputes over territorial claims and maritime resources are resolved peacefully and according to international law.

As the Arctic becomes more accessible due to shrinking ice, there are concerns about potential geopolitical tensions and competition over resources. Some nations are vying for expanded access and control over Arctic shipping routes and resource-rich areas. Maintaining a stable and cooperative geopolitical environment is essential to preventing conflicts and fostering regional cooperation.

Commercial shipping in the Arctic is another aspect that requires careful governance. While the opening of new shipping routes, such as the Northern Sea Route, presents economic opportunities, it also raises safety and environmental concerns. Effective regulations and collaboration among nations are necessary to ensure safe navigation, prevent accidents, and respond to potential emergencies.

The role of the private sector in Arctic development and governance is significant. Companies engaged in resource extraction, shipping, tourism, and research have a responsibility to adhere to environmental standards and engage in sustainable practices. Collaborating with local communities and indigenous peoples can foster positive and mutually beneficial relationships.

As the Arctic continues to undergo rapid changes, it is essential to maintain a holistic approach to governance, taking into account the interconnectedness of environmental, social, economic, and geopolitical factors. Balancing the interests and concerns of various stakeholders requires open dialogue, cooperation, and a commitment to safeguarding the Arctic's unique environment and the livelihoods of its inhabitants.

Greenland: The Land of Ice and Vikings

Nestled in the vast expanse of the Arctic, Greenland stands as a majestic and enigmatic land of ice, towering glaciers, and a rich history that traces back to the legendary Vikings. As the world's largest island, Greenland is a land of superlatives, where nature's forces have shaped a breathtaking landscape of fjords, icebergs, and ice sheets that cover about 80% of the island's surface.

Greenland's ice sheet is a marvel of nature, reaching immense heights of over two miles in some places. This massive ice sheet contains an estimated 2.6 million cubic kilometers of ice, making it one of the world's largest freshwater reserves. It plays a critical role in regulating global climate patterns and sea levels, capturing and storing vast amounts of freshwater that, if melted, could significantly impact the world's oceans.

The ice sheet is also a unique environment for scientific research. Scientists from around the globe come to Greenland to study its ice cores, which provide valuable insights into past climate conditions and help us better understand the Earth's history and future. These ice cores act as a time capsule, preserving ancient air bubbles that contain traces of greenhouse gases and other atmospheric components, providing valuable data for climate change research.

Greenland's icy landscapes are not only a scientific wonder but also a haven for adventure seekers and nature enthusiasts. Tourists flock to Greenland to witness the awe-inspiring beauty of its glaciers and icebergs, often taking boat tours to observe these floating ice giants as they break off from the glaciers and drift through the Arctic waters. The icebergs' hues of blue and white create a mesmerizing spectacle that captures the imagination and leaves visitors in awe of nature's grandeur.

Beyond its icy allure, Greenland has a rich cultural heritage that traces back over 4,500 years. The island was first inhabited by the ancestors of the modern-day Inuit people, who arrived from North America. These indigenous peoples developed a profound connection with the land and the sea, adapting their way of life to the harsh Arctic environment.

Greenland's history also intertwines with the legendary Norse explorers. The Vikings, led by Erik the Red, established colonies on the southwestern coast of Greenland around the 10th century. These settlements, including the famous Brattahlid, thrived for several centuries before mysteriously disappearing, leaving behind intriguing archaeological sites that continue to be a source of fascination and research.

Today, Greenland is an autonomous territory within the Kingdom of Denmark. While Greenlanders govern their domestic affairs, Denmark oversees defense and foreign policy matters. The island's political landscape has seen significant changes over the years, with discussions about potential independence generating debates among the population.

Greenland's population is relatively small, with around 56,000 inhabitants, most of whom live along the western coastline. The capital city, Nuuk, is home to the largest population and serves as Greenland's cultural and political hub. In addition to Danish, Greenlandic, an Inuit-Aleut language, is also spoken across the island.

Despite its vast natural resources, Greenland faces economic challenges due to its remote location and limited infrastructure. Traditional industries such as fishing and hunting still play a vital role in the economy, while tourism and mineral extraction have been emerging sectors of growth. The potential for mineral resources, including rare earth minerals, has attracted international interest, raising debates about the balance between economic development and environmental protection.

Climate change presents both opportunities and risks for Greenland. While melting ice and longer ice-free periods open up new economic possibilities, they also threaten the traditional ways of life for the indigenous communities. The effects of climate change, including coastal erosion and thawing permafrost, require adaptation strategies to protect communities and cultural heritage.

Greenland's unique combination of icy landscapes, rich history, and cultural heritage make it a captivating destination for explorers and adventurers alike. As the world continues to grapple with environmental challenges and a changing Arctic, Greenland remains a symbol of resilience, a land that continues to captivate the human spirit with its frozen wonders and storied past. It stands as a testament to the delicate balance between human activities and the pristine Arctic environment, urging us to embrace sustainability and preservation for the generations to come.

Svalbard: Norway's Arctic Gateway

Nestled between the Arctic Ocean, the Norwegian Sea, and the Greenland Sea, lies the stunning archipelago of Svalbard. This remote and rugged land is a territory of Norway and serves as its Arctic gateway, offering access to the vast and uncharted realms of the North.

Svalbard consists of several islands, with Spitsbergen being the largest and most populous. Despite its northern location, Svalbard enjoys a milder climate compared to other Arctic regions due to the influence of the Gulf Stream, which brings warmer waters and moderates temperatures.

The archipelago's history is rich and intertwined with Arctic exploration and the quest for resources. Norwegian whalers and hunters were among the first to venture into these icy waters, seeking the bounty of marine life that thrives in the Arctic. Over the centuries, Svalbard became a base for Arctic expeditions, attracting explorers from various nations keen on unlocking the secrets of the North.

In the early 20th century, Svalbard became an important center for coal mining. The discovery of coal deposits drew international attention, leading to the Svalbard Treaty of 1920. This treaty recognized Norwegian sovereignty over the archipelago while establishing the principle of equal access to economic activities for all signatory nations. Today, the treaty governs Svalbard's unique legal status, allowing citizens of signatory countries to reside and conduct business on the islands without a visa.

Longyearbyen, located on Spitsbergen, is the largest settlement in Svalbard and serves as its administrative center. Despite its small size, Longyearbyen is a vibrant community with modern amenities, research facilities, and a growing tourism industry. The University Centre in Svalbard (UNIS) offers courses and conducts research on Arctic-related topics, attracting students and scientists from around the world.

The Arctic wilderness of Svalbard is a haven for wildlife. Polar bears, reindeer, Arctic foxes, and various bird species inhabit the islands, making it a popular destination for wildlife enthusiasts and nature photographers. However, the presence of polar bears poses risks, and visitors are required to be cautious and take safety measures while exploring the archipelago's remote areas.

Svalbard's unique geography and climate also make it an excellent location for observing celestial phenomena such as the Northern Lights, also known as the Aurora Borealis. During the winter months, when the nights are long and the skies are clear, visitors have a chance to witness the mesmerizing dance of colorful lights in the Arctic skies.

Tourism is a growing industry in Svalbard, drawing travelers seeking unforgettable Arctic experiences. Activities such as dog sledding, ice caving, and boat tours to see glaciers and wildlife are popular among visitors. Cruise ships and expedition vessels frequent Svalbard's waters, allowing passengers to explore the awe-inspiring landscapes and remote corners of the Arctic.

Svalbard's proximity to the North Pole has also made it a base for scientific research. Numerous research stations and observatories dot the archipelago, studying various aspects of the Arctic environment, climate change, and polar ecosystems. The data collected from these research efforts contribute to our understanding of the Earth's changing climate and the impacts on the Arctic.

Despite its natural beauty and unique opportunities, Svalbard faces challenges due to the changing Arctic climate and increased human activities. The melting of the ice and permafrost poses risks to infrastructure, and efforts are underway to adapt and mitigate these effects. The management of tourism and resource extraction requires careful planning to ensure sustainable practices and preserve the fragile Arctic ecosystem.

As Norway's Arctic gateway, Svalbard embodies the spirit of exploration and the pursuit of knowledge in the Arctic realm. Its breathtaking landscapes, rich history, and scientific significance make it a place of intrigue and wonder for those seeking to venture into the Arctic's icy embrace.

The Faroe Islands: Where Nature Rules

Nestled in the North Atlantic Ocean, halfway between Iceland and Norway, lies a hidden gem of rugged beauty and untamed nature - the Faroe Islands. This remote archipelago of 18 volcanic islands is a land of contrasts, where towering cliffs meet serene fjords, and lush green landscapes blend seamlessly with the dramatic forces of the North Atlantic.

Despite their small size and relative isolation, the Faroe Islands boast a rich and vibrant history that dates back to the Viking Age. The islands were first settled by Norse settlers around the 9th century, and their influence can still be seen in the Faroese culture, language, and traditions. Today, the Faroese language, a Nordic language derived from Old Norse, is spoken by the islanders and serves as a symbol of their unique identity.

The Faroese people have a strong connection to the land and the sea, with fishing and sheep farming being the traditional mainstays of their economy. The islands' fertile valleys provide grazing land for sheep, which have become an integral part of Faroese life, providing not only sustenance but also wool for traditional Faroese sweaters known as "lopapeysa."

Nature is at the heart of the Faroese way of life, and the islanders have a deep respect for the environment. The stunning landscapes and wildlife offer ample opportunities for outdoor activities and exploration. Hiking is a popular pastime, with trails leading to breathtaking viewpoints and hidden gems tucked away in the hills. The challenging terrain and ever-changing weather add an element of adventure to each expedition.

One of the most iconic symbols of the Faroe Islands is the puffin, a colorful and endearing seabird that thrives in the cliffs and grassy slopes of the islands. Puffin colonies can be found scattered across the archipelago, and witnessing these charming birds in their natural habitat is a highlight for many visitors.

The Faroe Islands' dramatic landscapes are further accentuated by their ever-changing weather. It is said that in the Faroes, you can experience all four seasons in one day. Fog and mist often shroud the islands, adding an air of mystery and enchantment to the surroundings. The weather can be unpredictable, but it also brings a sense of authenticity and raw beauty to the Faroese experience.

In addition to its natural wonders, the Faroe Islands boast a unique cultural scene. The islands host a range of music festivals, art exhibitions, and traditional events that showcase Faroese talent and creativity. Faroese cuisine is also a point of pride, with an emphasis on locally sourced ingredients, including fresh fish and lamb. The Faroese national dish, "ræst kjøt," is made from fermented lamb that has been air-dried for several months, reflecting the islanders' resourceful approach to preserving food in the past.

While the Faroe Islands embrace their remote and untouched landscapes, they are not completely isolated from the world. Regular ferry services and flights connect the islands to neighboring countries, making them accessible to travelers seeking an authentic and off-the-beaten-path adventure.

However, the Faroese people are mindful of the delicate balance between preserving their unique environment and accommodating tourism. Sustainable tourism practices are increasingly emphasized to protect the fragile ecosystems and maintain the islands' pristine beauty for future generations to enjoy.

The Faroe Islands' respect for nature is also reflected in their sustainable fishing practices. The islands are known for their high-quality seafood, and efforts are made to ensure that fishing remains ecologically responsible and economically viable.

As you explore the Faroe Islands, you will find a land where nature reigns supreme, and the rhythm of life follows the cycles of the seasons and the ebb and flow of the tides. The Faroese people have forged a deep connection with their surroundings, and this connection is evident in their art, music, and daily lives. The Faroe Islands offer a unique opportunity to escape the hustle and bustle of modern life and immerse oneself in the beauty and tranquility of a land where nature rules.

Iceland: The Volcanic Heart of the Arctic

Welcome to the land of fire and ice, where the raw power of nature takes center stage - Iceland. This extraordinary island nation, situated in the North Atlantic Ocean, is a place of striking contrasts, where majestic glaciers coexist with bubbling geysers, and towering volcanoes shape the landscape.

Iceland is a land forged by volcanic activity, and its geothermal wonders are a testament to the immense forces at work beneath the Earth's surface. The island sits atop the Mid-Atlantic Ridge, a divergent tectonic boundary where the North American and Eurasian tectonic plates slowly drift apart. This unique geological setting makes Iceland a hotbed of geothermal activity, giving rise to geysers, hot springs, and bubbling mud pools that are a hallmark of the country.

One of Iceland's most famous geysers is the Great Geysir, from which the word "geyser" is derived. While the Great Geysir is now relatively inactive, its neighbor, Strokkur, erupts every few minutes, shooting hot water up to 100 feet into the air, delighting visitors with its natural spectacle.

Iceland's volcanic landscapes are further accentuated by its numerous glaciers. The country is home to several ice caps, the largest being Vatnajökull, covering an area roughly the size of the state of Connecticut. These massive ice formations hold a significant portion of Iceland's freshwater and are a vital source of many of the country's rivers.

The combination of glaciers and geothermal activity creates some of Iceland's most captivating natural wonders. Glacial lagoons, such as Jökulsárlón, are formed when melting icebergs drift into serene lakes, creating a surreal landscape of floating ice chunks in a stunning range of colors.

Iceland's volcanic heritage is also reflected in its dramatic coastlines and rocky cliffs. The basalt formations of Reynisfjara Beach and the sea stacks of Dyrhólaey are prime examples of the country's unique geological features. The interaction of volcanic activity and ocean waves has carved these breathtaking landscapes over thousands of years, leaving visitors awe-inspired by their beauty.

Volcanoes hold a prominent place in Iceland's history and folklore. The island is home to over 130 volcanoes, with some of the most infamous eruptions etched into the collective memory of the Icelandic people. One of the most significant eruptions in recent history was the eruption of Eyjafjallajökull in 2010. This eruption disrupted air travel across Europe, grounding flights and bringing attention to the power and unpredictability of Iceland's volcanoes.

While volcanic eruptions can be disruptive, they also contribute to Iceland's unique ecosystem. The nutrient-rich volcanic soil supports a vibrant array of flora and fauna, with hardy plants such as moss and lichen covering vast lava fields. Iceland's coastal waters are also rich in marine life, attracting whales, seals, and a variety of seabirds.

Iceland's geological wonders have not only shaped its landscape but also influenced its culture and traditions. The island's folklore is rife with stories of elves, trolls, and hidden people believed to inhabit the natural features of the land. Respect for nature and its mystical elements is deeply ingrained in Icelandic culture, adding an air of magic and mystique to the country's identity.

Iceland's geothermal energy has also become a valuable resource, providing heating and electricity to the population. The country's commitment to renewable energy sources has made it a global leader in sustainable practices, and geothermal power plays a significant role in reducing carbon emissions.

As you explore the volcanic heart of the Arctic, you will find a land of wonder and discovery, where the forces of nature continue to shape the world around us. From the icy glaciers to the fiery volcanoes, Iceland stands as a testament to the Earth's dynamic and ever-changing nature. Its geological wonders, vibrant culture, and breathtaking landscapes make it a destination like no other, captivating the hearts of travelers and igniting a lifelong fascination with this land of fire and ice.

Nunavut: Canada's Arctic Frontier

Venture into the vast and unexplored realm of Canada's Arctic frontier - Nunavut, a land of breathtaking beauty and cultural richness. Located in the northernmost reaches of Canada, Nunavut is the country's newest and largest territory, encompassing nearly two million square kilometers of pristine Arctic wilderness.

The creation of Nunavut as a distinct territory in 1999 marked a historic moment for the indigenous Inuit people. The territory's name, "Nunavut," translates to "our land" in Inuktitut, one of the official languages spoken by the Inuit. This act of self-governance acknowledges the deep connection the Inuit have to the land and their centuries-old traditions and way of life.

Nunavut is home to a small but resilient population, with most communities situated along the coastline due to the challenging terrain and harsh climate of the Arctic. The capital city, Iqaluit, located on Baffin Island, serves as the administrative hub and is the largest community in Nunavut. The Inuit people's cultural heritage is evident in every aspect of life in the territory, from art and music to language and traditional practices.

The landscapes of Nunavut are as diverse as they are awe-inspiring. Glaciers, icebergs, and fjords punctuate the coastline, while vast tundra and rugged mountains dominate the interior. The sheer size and unspoiled nature of the territory make it a paradise for outdoor enthusiasts, researchers, and adventurers seeking to connect with the Arctic wilderness.

The Arctic wildlife of Nunavut is equally impressive, with polar bears, walruses, narwhals, and beluga whales among the iconic species that call this region home. Nunavut is a vital habitat for migratory birds, providing nesting grounds and sustenance for countless species, including the colorful snow geese that migrate annually.

As a land of extreme seasons, Nunavut experiences both the midnight sun during the summer months and the polar nights in winter. During the summer solstice, the sun remains above the horizon for weeks, creating an ethereal phenomenon known as the "land of the midnight sun." Conversely, in the depths of winter, the sun disappears entirely, leaving the territory in prolonged darkness.

Nunavut's climate presents unique challenges and opportunities for its inhabitants. While the territory experiences cold temperatures throughout the year, the Arctic environment also offers an abundance of resources that sustain traditional hunting, fishing, and gathering practices for the Inuit people.

The Inuit culture and traditions are deeply intertwined with the land and sea. Inuktitut, the Inuit language, is an integral part of daily life and serves as a vessel for passing down knowledge and ancestral stories. Traditional practices, such as dog sledding, kayaking, and throat singing, continue to be celebrated and preserved, ensuring the Inuit heritage remains a vital part of Nunavut's identity.

The territory's vastness and isolation also make it an ideal location for scientific research. Scientists from around the world come to Nunavut to study various aspects of the Arctic environment, including climate change, marine life, and the impact of human activities on the fragile ecosystems.

Despite its natural beauty and cultural significance, Nunavut faces unique challenges. The remoteness and limited infrastructure present difficulties in accessing healthcare, education, and economic opportunities for many communities. The impact of climate change also threatens the traditional way of life for the Inuit people, as melting ice and changing weather patterns disrupt hunting and fishing practices.

Alaska: America's Last Frontier

In the far reaches of the North American continent lies a land of extraordinary beauty and untamed wilderness - Alaska, America's last frontier. This vast and rugged state is unlike any other in the United States, boasting a diverse landscape that ranges from towering mountains to sprawling tundra and icy glaciers.

Alaska's history is rich and steeped in adventure. Native Alaskans, including the Inupiaq, Yup'ik, and Athabaskan people, have inhabited the region for thousands of years, making it their home long before European explorers arrived. The Russian Empire established its presence in Alaska in the 18th century, and it wasn't until 1867 that the territory was purchased by the United States in what was famously known as the "Alaska Purchase."

The state's nickname, "The Last Frontier," is a testament to its vast size and relative isolation. With over 663,000 square miles of land, Alaska is the largest state in the United States and is larger than many countries. Despite its immense size, Alaska is one of the least populated states, with a population density far lower than the national average.

Alaska's landscapes are a mesmerizing blend of natural wonders. The state is home to Denali, formerly known as Mount McKinley, the highest peak in North America, soaring over 20,000 feet above sea level. The Alaska Range, which houses Denali, is just one of the state's many mountain ranges, each with its unique character and allure.

Glaciers are a defining feature of Alaska's geography, and the state is home to more than 100,000 glaciers, ranging from small icefields to colossal rivers of ice. The Mendenhall Glacier near Juneau and the Hubbard Glacier near Yakutat are among the most accessible and awe-inspiring, drawing visitors from around the world to witness their grandeur.

The coastline of Alaska stretches for over 6,600 miles, bordered by the Pacific Ocean and the Bering Sea. This extensive coastline provides a rich marine habitat, attracting diverse marine life, including humpback whales, orcas, sea otters, and countless seabirds. The Inside Passage, a network of fjords and channels, offers a stunning route for cruise ships and small vessels to explore Alaska's coastal wonders.

Alaska's wildlife is legendary, with opportunities for observing bears, moose, wolves, and bald eagles in their natural habitat. Katmai National Park and Preserve, in particular, is renowned for its brown bear population and the spectacular bear-watching experiences it offers.

The state's climate varies significantly across its expanse. Coastal regions tend to have milder temperatures due to the moderating influence of the ocean, while the interior experiences more extreme temperatures, with frigid winters and warm summers. The Arctic region of Alaska, located above the Arctic Circle, is known for its harsh winters and the unique phenomenon of the midnight sun during the summer months.

Alaska's economy relies heavily on natural resources, including oil, gas, minerals, and fish. The Prudhoe Bay oil field on the North Slope is one of the largest oil fields in North America and plays a crucial role in Alaska's economy. Fishing is also a significant industry, with the state providing a large portion of the nation's seafood.

The indigenous cultures of Alaska remain an essential part of the state's identity. Native Alaskan traditions and languages continue to thrive, with many communities preserving their unique heritage through art, storytelling, and traditional practices.

As you journey into America's last frontier, you will encounter a land of vast landscapes and infinite possibilities. Alaska's wild beauty and untouched wilderness make it a paradise for outdoor enthusiasts and adventurers seeking to immerse themselves in the heart of nature. The state's commitment to preserving its natural heritage and fostering a spirit of conservation ensures that Alaska will remain an untamed treasure for generations to come, a place where the true spirit of the frontier lives on in all its splendor.

Northern Russia: The Vast Arctic Expanse

Prepare to explore the remote and enigmatic realm of Northern Russia, a land of superlatives and extremes that stretches across the Arctic expanse. This vast region encompasses a significant portion of the Arctic Circle, with landscapes that range from icy tundra and rugged mountains to dense forests and frozen seas.

Northern Russia's history is deeply intertwined with the Arctic's challenges and opportunities. The Russian Empire's expansion into the north began in the 16th century, driven by the search for valuable furs and new trade routes. Over the centuries, Russian settlers and explorers gradually pushed northward, establishing settlements and trading outposts along the Arctic coasts.

One of the defining features of Northern Russia is its sheer size. This vast expanse covers an area that spans several time zones, making it one of the largest territories in the world. It encompasses the Russian Far East, the vast Siberian hinterlands, and the sparsely populated Arctic territories that extend to the borders with Norway and Finland.

The Russian Far East is a treasure trove of natural wonders and diverse ecosystems. It is home to the Kamchatka Peninsula, a land of fiery volcanoes, geysers, and hot springs, earning it the nickname "The Land of Fire and Ice." Kamchatka is also a haven for wildlife, with populations of brown bears, reindeer, and countless species of birds.

Siberia, often associated with frigid temperatures and harsh conditions, is the heart of Northern Russia. This massive region stretches across the Asian continent, with some of the world's longest rivers, including the Ob, Yenisei, and Lena rivers, flowing through its vast territories. Siberia's subarctic climate means bitterly cold winters, but also warm and pleasant summers.

One of the most famous features of Northern Russia is Lake Baikal, the world's deepest and oldest freshwater lake. Located in southern Siberia, this natural wonder contains about 20% of the world's unfrozen freshwater reserve and boasts a unique and diverse ecosystem, with many plant and animal species found nowhere else on Earth.

Northern Russia's Arctic territories are characterized by their extreme conditions and remote isolation. The Yamal Peninsula, located in the Russian Arctic, is known for its vast gas reserves and reindeer herding traditions of the indigenous Nenets people. The indigenous cultures in the Arctic regions of Russia, such as the Nenets, the Khanty, and the Chukchi, have lived in harmony with the land and its resources for millennia.

The Northern Sea Route, a historic Arctic shipping route, is becoming increasingly accessible due to the melting sea ice caused by climate change. This route connects the Atlantic and Pacific Oceans, providing a shorter passage between Europe and Asia. It offers significant economic opportunities for Russia and other nations seeking faster and more efficient trade routes.

Northern Russia is also home to some of the coldest inhabited places on Earth. The town of Oymyakon holds the record for the lowest officially recorded temperature in a permanently inhabited location, with temperatures plummeting to as low as minus 90 degrees Fahrenheit.

The region's vast wilderness and unique conditions make it a paradise for adventure seekers and nature enthusiasts. The Northern Lights, also known as the Aurora Borealis, frequently illuminate the Arctic skies, painting breathtaking displays of color and light.

Despite its remote and challenging nature, Northern Russia plays a crucial role in global geopolitics and resource extraction. The region is rich in natural resources, including oil, gas, minerals, and timber, making it a significant player in the global energy and raw materials markets.

Arctic Research Stations: Advancing Science in Isolation

In the remote and frozen expanses of the Arctic, a group of brave and dedicated scientists embark on extraordinary journeys of discovery. These intrepid researchers reside in Arctic research stations, outposts of human civilization surrounded by vast ice and frigid waters. Operating in extreme isolation, these stations play a critical role in advancing our understanding of the Arctic's complex ecosystems and the impact of climate change on our planet. Arctic research stations are strategically located across the region, from Alaska to Greenland, from Russia to Canada. Each station serves as a base for a diverse range of scientific studies, covering everything from atmospheric research and glaciology to marine biology and archaeology.

The isolation and harsh conditions of Arctic research stations pose unique challenges for scientists and support staff. Many of these stations can only be reached by air or ice-breaking ships, making resupply missions infrequent and weather-dependent. Despite the logistical difficulties, these remote outposts are essential for collecting valuable data and conducting long-term observations in one of the most critical regions affected by climate change. One of the most well-known research stations in the Arctic is the Barrow Atmospheric Baseline Observatory (BRW) in Utqiaġvik, Alaska. BRW is part of the Global Atmosphere Watch program, monitoring greenhouse gases and atmospheric aerosols to better understand their role in global climate change. Its location at the northernmost tip of Alaska makes it an ideal site for studying the composition of the Arctic atmosphere.

In Canada, the Polar Environment Atmospheric Research Laboratory (PEARL) is perched on a remote plateau in Eureka, Nunavut. PEARL focuses on researching the ozone layer, atmospheric particles, and climate change effects in the Arctic. The station's high altitude and Arctic location make it an important vantage point for monitoring the Earth's upper atmosphere. In Greenland, the Summit Camp is a research station located at the highest point of the Greenland Ice Sheet. Scientists at Summit Camp study ice cores, which contain valuable information about past climate conditions. By analyzing these ice cores, researchers can reconstruct historical climate changes and gain insights into the Earth's climate system. Another remarkable research station is the Amundsen-Scott South Pole Station, located at the geographic South Pole. While not in the Arctic, this station's extreme isolation and harsh conditions parallel those of Arctic research stations. Amundsen-Scott focuses on a wide range of research, including glaciology, astronomy, and atmospheric science, and its location provides valuable data for understanding global climate patterns.

Life in an Arctic research station is an exercise in adaptation and teamwork. Scientists and support staff live and work in close quarters, forming tight-knit communities. They endure months of darkness during polar nights and experience the surreal phenomenon of the midnight sun during summer. Survival skills, self-sufficiency, and resilience are vital attributes for those working in these extreme environments. The research conducted in Arctic stations is vital for understanding the impacts of climate change on the Arctic region and beyond. The Arctic is warming at a rate twice as fast as the global average, leading to melting ice, rising sea levels, and shifts in ecosystems. The data collected in Arctic research stations contributes to global climate models and informs policymakers about the urgent need for action to mitigate climate change. Moreover, Arctic research stations are crucial for advancing our understanding of the Arctic's unique biodiversity. Marine biologists study Arctic marine life, including polar bears, seals, whales, and a variety of fish species, to unravel the intricate relationships between these species and their icy habitats.

As climate change accelerates, the Arctic research community faces new challenges and uncertainties. The Arctic's rapidly changing environment necessitates adaptive and innovative research methods. Researchers are increasingly collaborating with indigenous communities, whose traditional knowledge and observations are invaluable for understanding the Arctic's evolving ecosystems.

Arctic research stations stand as beacons of scientific inquiry in the face of extreme isolation and adversity. Through their dedication and discoveries, these stations provide us with a deeper understanding of the Arctic's delicate balance and its crucial role in shaping the global climate. As the Arctic continues to transform, these outposts of human endeavor remain steadfast in their pursuit of knowledge, serving as a testament to the resilience of the human spirit and the importance of preserving the Arctic for future generations.

Arctic Tourism: Experiencing the North Pole

Embark on a thrilling adventure to the North Pole, where Arctic tourism offers a once-in-a-lifetime opportunity to witness the majestic beauty and wild wonders of the Arctic. As one of the world's last frontiers, the Arctic lures intrepid travelers seeking to immerse themselves in a world of ice and snow, a world where polar bears roam, and the midnight sun dances in the sky.

Arctic tourism has grown in popularity over the years, as travelers seek to explore this remote and pristine region. The allure of the Arctic lies in its untouched landscapes, its unique wildlife, and the chance to witness natural phenomena that are rarely seen anywhere else on Earth.

One of the primary ways tourists venture into the Arctic is through expedition cruises. Specialized ships navigate through icy waters, taking travelers on an unforgettable journey along the coastlines of Alaska, Canada, Greenland, Norway, and Russia. These cruises offer a safe and comfortable way to explore the Arctic's beauty, with onboard experts providing insights into the region's ecology, history, and cultures.

A highlight of Arctic cruises is the chance to witness majestic icebergs and glaciers up close. The colossal walls of ice calving into the sea create a symphony of sights and sounds, a spectacle that leaves travelers in awe of the forces of nature. Glacier hiking and kayaking are popular activities that allow tourists to get even closer to these icy giants.

For those seeking a more immersive Arctic experience, land-based tours are available, offering an opportunity to step foot on the frozen tundra and explore the Arctic wilderness on foot. These tours often include visits to remote Inuit communities, where travelers can learn about the traditional way of life and the challenges of living in such a harsh environment.

The Arctic's wildlife is a significant draw for tourists, and sightings of polar bears, beluga whales, walruses, and seabirds are common. In Svalbard, Norway, polar bear spotting is a popular activity, as this archipelago is home to one of the densest populations of polar bears in the world.

One of the most sought-after experiences in Arctic tourism is witnessing the mesmerizing Northern Lights, or Aurora Borealis. The Arctic's high latitude and long winter nights make it an ideal location for viewing this natural light show, where vibrant colors dance across the night sky.

In the summer months, the Arctic experiences the phenomenon of the midnight sun, where the sun remains above the horizon for weeks. This creates endless opportunities for adventure and exploration under the soft glow of the midnight sun, a surreal experience that cannot be replicated anywhere else on Earth.

Arctic tourism, however, comes with a responsibility to preserve this delicate and pristine environment. The impact of increased tourism on Arctic ecosystems and indigenous cultures is a concern that needs careful management. Tour operators are increasingly working with local communities to ensure sustainable tourism practices that respect the Arctic's unique heritage and environment.

As climate change continues to impact the Arctic, responsible tourism becomes even more critical. Observing the effects of melting ice and the changing Arctic landscapes can provide visitors with a deeper understanding of the urgency to protect this fragile region for future generations.

Arctic tourism opens a gateway to a world of unparalleled beauty and wonder, a world that remains largely untouched by human development. From the icy wilderness to the warm hospitality of the Arctic's indigenous peoples, the North Pole offers a once-in-a-lifetime experience that will forever leave a mark on the hearts and minds of those who venture to its frozen shores. As we explore the Arctic, let us also take with us a sense of stewardship, preserving this extraordinary place for generations to come, so that the magic of the Arctic will continue to inspire and captivate the souls of those who dare to venture into its icy embrace.

Dogsledding and Snowmobile Safaris: Arctic Adventures

In the Arctic, where the icy landscapes stretch as far as the eye can see, a world of thrilling adventures awaits those who seek to explore the frozen wilderness. Among the most iconic and exhilarating activities in the Arctic are dogsledding and snowmobile safaris, providing travelers with a unique opportunity to experience the Arctic like a true explorer.

Dogsledding has been a traditional mode of transportation for indigenous Arctic communities for thousands of years. Today, it remains an essential part of the Arctic way of life and a beloved tourist attraction for visitors seeking an authentic Arctic experience.

Dogsledding is an art that requires a deep connection between the musher (the person driving the sled) and their team of sled dogs. The bond between musher and dogs is built on trust, as these intelligent and hardworking animals rely on their human companion for guidance and care. Sled dogs, such as Alaskan Malamutes, Siberian Huskies, and Greenland Dogs, are bred for endurance, strength, and agility, making them perfectly suited for navigating the Arctic terrain.

Snow-covered trails wind through majestic snowy landscapes, passing frozen lakes and dense forests. The rhythmic sound of paws hitting the snow and the soft swishing of the sled runners create a serene and magical atmosphere. Dogsledding allows travelers to immerse themselves in the tranquility of the Arctic wilderness, where the only sounds are the crunch of snow underfoot and the occasional howl of the wind.

For those seeking a faster and more exhilarating Arctic adventure, snowmobile safaris provide an adrenaline-pumping experience. Snowmobiles, also known as snow machines, offer a thrilling way to cover vast distances in the Arctic's frozen expanses, providing access to remote and otherwise inaccessible areas.

Snowmobile safaris are particularly popular in regions like Lapland in Finland, where the landscape is dotted with frozen lakes and snow-capped forests. Tourists can zip through the Arctic wilderness, feeling the rush of icy wind against their faces as they explore the untamed beauty of the Arctic.

As with any Arctic adventure, safety is of utmost importance when engaging in dogsledding and snowmobile safaris. Tour operators provide necessary safety equipment and guidelines to ensure that travelers can enjoy their experiences while minimizing risks to both themselves and the fragile Arctic environment.

Dogsledding and snowmobile safaris not only offer thrilling adventures but also provide an opportunity to connect with Arctic culture and history. Many tours incorporate visits to indigenous communities, where travelers can learn about the traditional methods of dogsledding and gain insights into the timeless wisdom of Arctic peoples.

These Arctic adventures are not limited to seasoned adventurers; they are accessible to people of all ages and skill levels. Guided tours cater to various preferences, from short introductory rides to multi-day expeditions. Some tours even include overnight stays in cozy wilderness cabins, allowing travelers to witness the beauty of the Arctic night skies and maybe even catch a glimpse of the Northern Lights.

Moreover, dogsledding and snowmobile safaris are sustainable forms of tourism, as they have a minimal impact on the fragile Arctic environment. These activities respect the natural rhythm of the Arctic and the traditions of the indigenous peoples who have lived in harmony with the land for generations.

Whether you choose to glide through the Arctic tundra on a dogsled or zip across frozen lakes on a snowmobile, these Arctic adventures will leave you with memories that last a lifetime. In the Arctic, the spirit of exploration and the call of the wild beckon, inviting you to embrace the magic of this frozen wonderland and discover the true meaning of adventure in the heart of the Arctic.

Glamping in the Arctic: Luxuries in the Cold

In the heart of the Arctic, where the wilderness meets the icy horizon, a new form of adventure has emerged - glamping in the Arctic. Combining the thrill of wilderness exploration with the comforts of luxury accommodations, glamping offers a unique and unforgettable experience for travelers seeking to immerse themselves in the beauty of the Arctic without compromising on comfort.

Glamping, short for "glamorous camping," takes camping to a whole new level. It allows adventurers to connect with nature while enjoying modern amenities and personalized services. In the Arctic, glamping offers a surreal blend of untouched landscapes, starry skies, and the warm embrace of cozy accommodations.

Unlike traditional camping, where travelers set up their tents and rough it in the wilderness, glamping provides stylish and well-appointed accommodations, often in the form of heated safari-style tents, igloos, or luxury cabins. These accommodations are equipped with comfortable beds, plush bedding, and sometimes even en-suite bathrooms, ensuring that guests can retreat to a warm and inviting space after a day of Arctic exploration.

One of the most popular glamping destinations in the Arctic is Iceland, where travelers can stay in luxury geodesic domes with transparent ceilings. These unique domes offer panoramic views of the surrounding landscapes during the day and the dancing Northern Lights at night, creating an otherworldly and magical experience.

In Finland's Lapland, glamping options range from private glass-roofed cabins to luxury wilderness lodges. Guests can indulge in Nordic-inspired spa treatments, relax in saunas, and savor gourmet meals prepared with locally sourced ingredients. These luxurious accommodations blend seamlessly with the Arctic wilderness, allowing guests to feel intimately connected with the stunning natural surroundings.

The glamping experience extends beyond the accommodations. Activities are tailored to provide guests with a taste of Arctic adventure, whether it's dogsledding through snow-covered forests, ice fishing on frozen lakes, or hiking through pristine landscapes. Experienced guides lead these excursions, ensuring that guests can safely explore the Arctic's wonders while learning about its unique ecosystems and wildlife.

In Greenland, glamping offers an opportunity to witness colossal glaciers up close and hear the gentle creaking and groaning of the ice as it moves. Guests can also kayak among icebergs, experiencing the serenity and grandeur of the Arctic seascape.

One of the key appeals of glamping in the Arctic is the chance to witness the Northern Lights. Many glamping accommodations are strategically located in regions with excellent Aurora visibility, offering guests a front-row seat to this breathtaking natural light show.

While glamping in the Arctic provides luxury and comfort, it also encourages responsible and sustainable tourism practices. Operators focus on minimizing their environmental impact, utilizing renewable energy sources, and supporting local communities. Many glamping experiences also provide opportunities for cultural immersion, allowing guests to interact with indigenous communities and learn about their traditional way of life.

As with any adventure in the Arctic, glamping requires preparation and awareness of the challenges of the cold and remote environment. Guests are provided with appropriate clothing and gear to stay warm and comfortable during their stay.

Glamping in the Arctic offers a chance to embrace the spirit of exploration and discovery while being enveloped in the lap of luxury. It is an experience that transcends ordinary travel, allowing guests to forge a deep connection with the Arctic's wild beauty and experience the true essence of Arctic adventure. Whether you're seeking a romantic escape, a family vacation, or a solo journey of self-discovery, glamping in the Arctic promises a once-in-a-lifetime experience that will stay with you forever. So, come and embark on this extraordinary Arctic adventure, where luxuries meet the cold, and where the magic of the Arctic awaits to captivate your heart and soul.

Arctic Cruises: Navigating Frozen Waters

Welcome aboard the adventure of a lifetime as we set sail on Arctic cruises, navigating through frozen waters to explore one of the world's most remote and captivating regions. The Arctic, with its icy landscapes, majestic glaciers, and abundant wildlife, beckons intrepid travelers to embark on a journey like no other.

Arctic cruises offer a unique and unforgettable way to experience the vastness and beauty of the Arctic, where the frozen seas hold tales of exploration and discovery. Unlike other cruises, Arctic expeditions are not about luxury and opulence; they are about embracing the spirit of adventure and immersing oneself in the wonders of nature.

The journey begins in countries like Norway, Greenland, Canada, and Russia, where specialized expedition vessels await to carry travelers through the icy waters. These ships are specially designed to navigate the challenging conditions of the Arctic, equipped with ice-strengthened hulls and advanced technology to ensure safe passage through frozen waters.

As the ship departs from port, passengers are greeted by a sense of anticipation and excitement. The Arctic's icy embrace lies ahead, promising encounters with polar bears, Arctic foxes, whales, and a myriad of seabirds. Each day brings new adventures, as the ship cruises through intricate fjords, passes towering icebergs, and navigates between floating pack ice.

Expert guides and naturalists accompany travelers on their Arctic expedition, providing in-depth knowledge about the region's history, wildlife, and geology. These experts share their passion for the Arctic, enriching the experience with captivating stories of explorers who braved these frozen waters centuries ago.

One of the highlights of Arctic cruises is the chance to witness majestic glaciers calving into the sea. The thunderous crash as ice breaks free from the glacier's face is both awe-inspiring and humbling, a reminder of the Arctic's ever-changing and dynamic nature.

In the summer months, the Arctic comes alive with an explosion of life. The midnight sun graces the horizon, bathing the landscape in a soft golden glow. It is a time of abundance as Arctic wildlife takes advantage of the brief but bountiful Arctic summer. Polar bears roam the ice, while humpback whales breach the surface of the Arctic seas, putting on a show for lucky onlookers.

Arctic cruises also provide opportunities for unforgettable shore excursions. Travelers can step foot on Arctic islands and witness the hardy flora that manages to survive in these extreme conditions. Exploring the tundra on foot, accompanied by experienced guides, offers a chance to connect intimately with the Arctic's delicate ecosystems.

The Arctic's indigenous cultures add depth and richness to the expedition experience. Some Arctic cruises include visits to Inuit communities, where guests can learn about traditional practices, art, and ways of life that have endured for generations.

Despite the allure and magic of the Arctic, it is a region that faces significant challenges. Climate change is rapidly altering the Arctic environment, with rising temperatures and melting ice affecting both wildlife and human communities. Responsible Arctic cruises prioritize sustainability and conservation, striving to minimize their impact on this delicate and pristine ecosystem.

Arctic cruises are not just about witnessing the Arctic's beauty; they are about fostering a deeper understanding and appreciation for this unique corner of the world. The experience of navigating frozen waters and witnessing the Arctic's splendor leaves a lasting impression on travelers, inspiring them to become advocates for the protection of this fragile region.

Inuit Heritage Centers: Preserving Arctic Culture

In the vast and remote expanse of the Arctic, the Inuit people have thrived for thousands of years, their rich cultural heritage woven into the fabric of this frozen landscape. To honor and preserve this ancient heritage, Inuit Heritage Centers have emerged as vital institutions, serving as repositories of knowledge, history, and tradition.

The Inuit, a remarkable Indigenous group, have inhabited the Arctic regions of Canada, Greenland, Alaska, and parts of Russia for millennia. They possess a deep understanding of the Arctic's unique environment, developed over generations of living in harmony with the land and sea. Their knowledge of survival, hunting, fishing, and navigation is unparalleled, and their artistic expressions and cultural practices reflect a profound connection with their surroundings.

Inuit Heritage Centers stand as living testimonies to the resilience and creativity of the Inuit people. These centers are dedicated to preserving and celebrating the diverse aspects of Inuit culture, from traditional art forms such as carving, printmaking, and beadwork, to storytelling, song, and dance. Through the preservation and exhibition of their art and artifacts, these centers showcase the Inuit's talent and creativity, offering visitors a glimpse into their remarkable world.

One of the essential roles of Inuit Heritage Centers is to act as custodians of oral history and storytelling. The Inuit have an ancient tradition of passing down knowledge through storytelling, with elders serving as the keepers of wisdom. At these centers, visitors have the privilege of listening to these captivating narratives, learning about Inuit history, myths, and legends, and gaining insight into the Inuit way of life.

Language plays a crucial role in Inuit culture, and these heritage centers play a significant role in language preservation. Many Inuit communities are multilingual, with different dialects spoken across the Arctic. Inuit Heritage Centers are actively involved in language revitalization efforts, offering language classes and resources to ensure that the Inuit languages thrive and continue to be a vital part of their culture.

The Inuit are renowned for their skill in crafting intricate and awe-inspiring art, often using materials sourced from the Arctic environment, such as stone, bone, and ivory. At these centers, visitors can marvel at the beauty and craftsmanship of Inuit art and even purchase authentic pieces, supporting local artisans and ensuring the continuation of these artistic traditions.

Inuit Heritage Centers also serve as community gathering spaces, where locals and visitors can come together to celebrate festivals, conduct ceremonies, and share their culture with the world. These centers host cultural events, workshops, and performances that highlight the vibrancy and diversity of Inuit culture, fostering a sense of pride and identity among the Inuit community.

Furthermore, Inuit Heritage Centers play a critical role in fostering cross-cultural understanding and appreciation. Visitors from around the globe can engage with the Inuit's unique way of life, gaining a deeper understanding of their relationship with the land, wildlife, and each other. These cultural exchanges create opportunities for dialogue, empathy, and respect, bridging the gap between different worlds and fostering a sense of global interconnectedness.

In recent years, there has been a growing interest in Indigenous knowledge and cultural heritage worldwide. Inuit Heritage Centers play an essential role in this movement, not only preserving the past but also shaping the future by empowering the Inuit to reclaim their cultural identity and assert their rights as Indigenous peoples.

Preserving Arctic culture is more critical now than ever, as the Arctic faces unprecedented challenges due to climate change and globalization. Inuit Heritage Centers stand as beacons of hope and resilience, reminding us of the enduring spirit of the Inuit people and the need to protect the Arctic's delicate ecosystems and cultural heritage for generations to come.

Arctic Festivals: Celebrating Life in the Cold

In the frozen lands of the Arctic, where winters are long and harsh, the Inuit and other Arctic communities have developed a rich tapestry of festivals to celebrate life and the changing seasons. These festivals are a testament to the resilience and spirit of the people who call the Arctic home, embracing the cold with warmth and joy.

One of the most eagerly awaited festivals in the Arctic is the Midwinter Festival, also known as the Winter Solstice. As the longest night of the year approaches, communities come together to celebrate the return of the sun and the promise of longer days. This festival is marked by lively gatherings, feasts, traditional dances, and storytelling. It is a time to honor ancestors, seek blessings for the new year, and express gratitude for the gifts of the Arctic land and sea.

The Whale Festival is another prominent celebration in the Arctic, particularly in Greenland and Canada's Arctic communities. It is a tribute to the majestic marine mammals that play a vital role in Arctic life. As the whales return to their summer feeding grounds, locals honor their presence with festivities, drum dances, and rituals. The festival also serves as an opportunity to raise awareness about the conservation of these magnificent creatures and their significance to the Arctic ecosystem.

In Alaska, the World Eskimo-Indian Olympics (WEIO) brings together Indigenous athletes from various Arctic communities for a week-long event celebrating traditional games and sports. The WEIO features events such as the blanket toss, where participants are thrown high into the air by a group holding a large blanket, and the knuckle hop, a test of endurance and skill. This festival showcases the physical prowess and cultural heritage of the Arctic's Indigenous peoples.

The Inuit have a strong connection to their ancestors and often hold festivals to honor them. Ancestor Day is a significant event where families come together to pay respects to their forebears, share stories, and participate in drumming ceremonies. It is a time to remember and celebrate the wisdom and legacy of those who came before, ensuring that their traditions and values continue to shape the community.

The return of migratory birds signals the arrival of spring in the Arctic, and the Arctic Bird Festival is a vibrant celebration of their return. Birdwatchers and nature enthusiasts gather to observe the spectacular array of avian species that grace the Arctic skies during this season. It is a time to marvel at the resilience of these winged travelers and their vital role in the Arctic ecosystem.

Another festival that reflects the Arctic's deep cultural ties to nature is the Northern Lights Festival. As the Aurora Borealis dances across the night sky, communities gather to witness this celestial display. The festival features art exhibitions, music performances, and storytelling sessions, all inspired by the enchanting beauty of the Northern Lights.

Throughout the Arctic, the summer brings the opportunity for hunting and gathering, and the Hunting and Harvest Festival celebrates the bounty of the land and sea. This festival is a time to share traditional foods, such as seal, whale, caribou, and fish, and to give thanks for the sustenance provided by the Arctic environment.

In Russia's Arctic regions, the Nenets people hold the Reindeer Herder's Festival, a tribute to their nomadic way of life and their deep bond with reindeer. The festival showcases reindeer racing, herding competitions, and displays of intricate reindeer herding gear. It is a testament to the skills and knowledge of the Nenets in navigating the Arctic tundra with their reindeer herds.

The celebrations in the Arctic are not just limited to specific festivals; there are numerous local events and gatherings that mark significant moments in the Arctic calendar. These events may include traditional dances, drumming circles, feasts, and ceremonies, all of which strengthen the bonds of community and cultural identity.

Arctic festivals are not only occasions of joy and merriment but also play a vital role in preserving and passing down cultural traditions to the younger generations. They serve as living expressions of the Arctic's unique heritage and provide opportunities for cultural exchange and understanding.

Whaling in the Arctic: Tradition vs. Conservation

In the vast expanse of the Arctic Ocean, whaling has been a centuries-old tradition for many Indigenous communities. For these communities, whaling is not just a means of sustenance but an integral part of their cultural identity and way of life. However, in recent times, the practice of whaling has come under scrutiny due to concerns about the conservation of whale populations and the impact of modern whaling techniques.

Whaling in the Arctic dates back thousands of years, with evidence of whaling activities found in archaeological sites across the region. For Indigenous communities like the Inuit, Yupik, and Chukchi, whaling is deeply rooted in their history, folklore, and spiritual beliefs. Whales are revered as majestic beings, and the hunt is carried out with respect and gratitude for the life that sustains the community.

Traditional whaling is a subsistence practice, meaning that it is primarily carried out to provide food and resources for the community's survival. Inuit whalers, for instance, use every part of the whale, from the meat for nourishment to the bones and skin for crafting tools, clothing, and art. The hunt is carefully regulated, and whalers adhere to cultural protocols and hunting traditions passed down through generations.

However, as modern technology and commercial interests encroach upon the Arctic, there has been a shift in the dynamics of whaling. Commercial whaling, driven by global demand for whale products, emerged in the 19th and 20th centuries, leading to a significant decline in whale populations worldwide. This indiscriminate hunting threatened the survival of many whale species and triggered international efforts to protect them.

In response to the conservation concerns, the International Whaling Commission (IWC) was established in 1946 to regulate whaling activities and ensure sustainable practices. Several whale species, including the blue whale, humpback whale, and gray whale, were designated as protected species, and their hunting was banned.

The IWC introduced quotas and moratoriums on whaling, limiting the number of whales that could be hunted each year to allow populations to recover. While some countries, like Japan, Norway, and Iceland, continue to conduct limited commercial whaling, the focus has shifted towards scientific research and cultural whaling practices by Indigenous communities.

For Arctic Indigenous communities, the clash between tradition and conservation is a complex issue. While they recognize the importance of preserving whale populations, they argue that their traditional whaling practices are sustainable and have minimal impact on whale populations. They contend that they have lived in harmony with the environment for centuries and that their knowledge of the whales and their behavior allows them to hunt in a way that respects the balance of nature.

The United States recognizes the cultural and subsistence significance of whaling for Alaska Native communities and has granted them special exemptions from the moratorium on whaling. The Marine Mammal Protection Act (MMPA) allows for subsistence hunting of bowhead and other whale species by Alaska Natives, ensuring the continuation of this cultural practice.

Despite these exemptions, the issue of whaling in the Arctic remains contentious. Conservationists argue that even subsistence whaling can put pressure on vulnerable whale populations, particularly in the face of other threats such as climate change and habitat degradation. They advocate for stricter regulations and monitoring to ensure that whaling practices remain sustainable.

Balancing tradition and conservation is an ongoing challenge, and it requires open dialogue and collaboration between Indigenous communities, governments, scientists, and conservation organizations. There is a growing recognition of the importance of Indigenous knowledge and involvement in conservation efforts, and many Arctic communities are actively engaged in research and monitoring to ensure the well-being of whale populations.

Arctic Mining: Resource Extraction in the North

In the remote and icy reaches of the Arctic, lies a treasure trove of natural resources, drawing the attention of industries seeking to unlock the region's potential. Arctic mining, though fraught with challenges, promises a wealth of minerals, fossil fuels, and precious metals that have become crucial components of the modern world. However, this pursuit of resources in the Arctic also raises concerns about environmental impacts, Indigenous rights, and the delicate balance between economic development and preservation.

The Arctic region is abundant in mineral deposits, including nickel, copper, zinc, lead, gold, and diamonds. These valuable resources have attracted mining companies from around the globe. Canada, Russia, Greenland, and Alaska are among the regions with significant mining operations. For example, Canada's Nunavut territory is rich in gold, diamonds, and iron ore, while Russia's Arctic holds vast reserves of natural gas and oil.

Mining in the Arctic is no small endeavor. The extreme weather, logistical challenges, and remote locations make operations complicated and expensive. The region's freezing temperatures, harsh winters, and ice-covered waters present formidable obstacles for transporting equipment and supplies. To overcome these challenges, companies must deploy specialized technology and infrastructure, such as ice-class vessels and heated pipelines.

The environmental impact of mining in the Arctic is a major concern. Fragile Arctic ecosystems, home to unique flora and fauna, are vulnerable to disruption. Spills and leaks from mining operations could have devastating consequences for the delicate balance of the region's ecology. Moreover, the melting ice caused by climate change is opening up new areas for mining, further heightening environmental risks.

Indigenous communities in the Arctic have voiced apprehensions about the encroachment of mining on their traditional lands. Many of these communities have subsisted on the land and waters for generations, and mining activities can threaten their way of life and cultural practices. The rights of Indigenous peoples to be consulted and participate in decision making regarding resource extraction are enshrined in international agreements, such as the United Nations Declaration on the Rights of Indigenous Peoples.

To address these concerns, some mining companies are engaging in dialogue with Indigenous communities and establishing partnerships to ensure sustainable practices and mutual benefits. Collaborative efforts between mining companies and Indigenous peoples aim to respect traditional knowledge, protect cultural heritage, and address socio-economic challenges in the Arctic.

Another contentious issue surrounding Arctic mining is the potential for conflict over territorial claims. The Arctic's vast resources have sparked competition among Arctic nations, leading to debates over sovereignty and control. The United Nations Convention on the Law of the Sea (UNCLOS) governs the allocation of resources beyond national borders, but disputes still arise, especially as the melting ice opens up new shipping routes and access to previously inaccessible resources.

While Arctic mining holds economic promise, it also presents significant ethical and environmental dilemmas. Striking a balance between resource extraction and environmental preservation is crucial. Technological advancements, environmental regulations, and corporate responsibility are vital in ensuring that mining operations in the Arctic are carried out responsibly and sustainably.

Arctic Energy: The Quest for Oil and Gas

In the icy expanse of the Arctic, beneath the frozen waters and permafrost, lies an immense reservoir of oil and natural gas, fueling the dreams of energy-hungry nations and energy companies. The Arctic's vast potential for oil and gas extraction has sparked a global quest for energy resources, with Arctic nations and multinational corporations vying to tap into this frozen treasure trove.

The Arctic is estimated to hold significant reserves of oil and gas, making it one of the last frontiers for hydrocarbon exploration. The United States Geological Survey (USGS) estimates that the Arctic region holds about 13% of the world's undiscovered oil and 30% of its undiscovered natural gas. These resources have become increasingly attractive as global demand for energy continues to rise.

The allure of Arctic oil and gas stems from its strategic significance and potential economic benefits. The region's proximity to major markets like Europe and Asia makes it an enticing source of energy for countries seeking to reduce their dependence on oil and gas from politically sensitive regions. Moreover, the melting ice in the Arctic, caused by climate change, is opening up new areas for exploration and production, making previously unreachable reserves accessible.

Several Arctic nations are actively involved in oil and gas exploration and production. Russia, for instance, has been a prominent player in Arctic energy development, with major projects in the Yamal Peninsula and the Russian Arctic shelf. Norway's offshore fields in the Barents Sea and Canada's exploration activities in the Beaufort Sea are also significant examples of Arctic energy development.

While the potential economic benefits of Arctic energy are evident, the pursuit of oil and gas in this delicate ecosystem raises numerous environmental concerns. The Arctic environment is exceptionally sensitive, and oil spills or gas leaks could have catastrophic consequences for marine life and delicate ecosystems. Additionally, increased human activity in the region, such as shipping and infrastructure development, can disturb wildlife and disrupt traditional Indigenous ways of life.

To address these concerns, international agreements and environmental regulations have been put in place to ensure responsible and sustainable energy development in the Arctic. The Arctic Council, comprising eight Arctic nations and Indigenous representatives, is an important forum for addressing environmental challenges and fostering cooperation in the region.

The exploration and production of Arctic oil and gas also pose unique technical and operational challenges. Harsh weather conditions, ice-covered waters, and remote locations make drilling and extraction complex and expensive. Companies must invest in specialized equipment and technology to operate in these extreme conditions.

In recent years, there has been growing attention to the potential impact of Arctic energy development on climate change. Extracting and burning fossil fuels from the Arctic can release significant greenhouse gas emissions, further contributing to global warming and accelerating the very processes that are opening up the region for resource extraction.

The pursuit of Arctic energy resources is not without opposition. Environmental groups, Indigenous communities, and concerned citizens worldwide advocate for a shift away from fossil fuels towards renewable energy sources to combat climate change and protect the Arctic ecosystem.

Arctic Diplomacy: International Relations in a Changing Climate

As the Arctic ice continues to melt, revealing new opportunities and challenges, the geopolitical landscape of the region is undergoing a significant transformation. The changing climate has opened up previously inaccessible shipping routes and vast natural resources, attracting the attention of Arctic and non-Arctic nations alike. In this era of shifting dynamics, Arctic diplomacy has become crucial in fostering cooperation, addressing shared concerns, and ensuring the preservation of the Arctic's delicate ecosystem.

The Arctic region is governed by a unique legal framework that includes international agreements and organizations aimed at promoting collaboration and addressing the concerns of Arctic nations. The Arctic Council, established in 1996, serves as a key platform for diplomatic engagement and cooperation. The Council includes eight Arctic nations—Canada, Denmark, Finland, Iceland, Norway, Russia, Sweden, and the United States—along with representatives from Indigenous Arctic communities.

The Council operates on consensus-based decision-making, allowing all member states to have an equal say in Arctic affairs. This cooperative approach has been instrumental in addressing environmental challenges, coordinating search and rescue efforts, and promoting scientific research in the region.

Climate change and its impact on the Arctic are among the most pressing concerns in Arctic diplomacy. The melting ice has raised the prospect of increased shipping and resource extraction, leading to potential disputes over territorial claims and resource ownership. At the same time, the changing climate poses a threat to Arctic communities, wildlife, and the stability of the global climate system.

To address these challenges, the Arctic nations have engaged in dialogues to develop cooperative strategies and agreements. The 2019 Finnish Chairmanship of the Arctic Council prioritized climate change and sustainable development, emphasizing the importance of transitioning to a low-carbon economy and strengthening resilience in the face of climate-related risks.

Non-Arctic nations have also shown growing interest in the Arctic. China, for example, has labeled itself a "near-Arctic state" and has sought to play a more significant role in the region's affairs. While non-Arctic nations do not have territorial claims in the Arctic, they have economic and strategic interests in the region, such as access to new shipping routes and resource extraction opportunities.

The inclusion of non-Arctic nations in Arctic discussions presents both opportunities and challenges. On one hand, their involvement can lead to increased investment in Arctic infrastructure and scientific research. On the other hand, it can also raise concerns about resource exploitation and potential tensions with Arctic nations.

To address these complexities, Arctic diplomacy focuses on fostering dialogue, promoting transparency, and seeking common ground. The 2013 Agreement on Enhancing International Arctic Scientific Cooperation, signed by all Arctic Council members, seeks to facilitate scientific research collaboration among nations to enhance understanding of the Arctic and its changing conditions.

The Arctic Council has also worked to address issues related to Indigenous rights and the involvement of Indigenous communities in Arctic governance. The inclusion of Indigenous representatives in the Council's work ensures that their voices and perspectives are taken into account in decision-making processes.

A Sustainable Future: Preserving the Arctic for Generations to Come

As the Arctic faces the dual challenges of climate change and increased human activity, the imperative for a sustainable future has never been more critical. Preserving this vast and pristine region is not just a matter of environmental responsibility but also a commitment to safeguarding the livelihoods of Indigenous communities and maintaining the delicate balance of the global ecosystem.

The Arctic is warming at a rate twice as fast as the global average, leading to the dramatic loss of sea ice, rising sea levels, and the disruption of weather patterns worldwide. The melting ice not only threatens Arctic wildlife and landscapes but also has far-reaching implications for coastal communities and low-lying regions around the world.

One of the most significant contributors to climate change is the burning of fossil fuels, which releases greenhouse gases into the atmosphere. As the Arctic opens up to resource extraction, the region's vast oil and gas reserves have become tempting targets for energy companies. However, harnessing these resources must be done responsibly, with stringent environmental regulations in place to minimize the impact on the fragile Arctic ecosystem.

The transition to renewable energy sources is a crucial step towards a sustainable Arctic future. Embracing clean energy alternatives like wind, solar, and hydroelectric power can reduce greenhouse gas emissions, mitigate climate change, and lessen the demand for Arctic oil and gas. Governments, businesses, and individuals must work together to invest in renewable energy infrastructure and promote energy efficiency in all aspects of life.

Arctic nations play a central role in shaping the region's sustainable future. Cooperation among these countries is vital to address shared challenges, establish protected areas, and implement conservation measures. The Arctic Council's role in fostering dialogue and collaboration is essential in developing sustainable policies and practices.

Preserving biodiversity is another crucial aspect of a sustainable Arctic future. The Arctic is home to a diverse range of flora and fauna, from majestic polar bears to elusive Arctic foxes and unique plant species. Protecting these habitats is not only essential for the survival of these creatures but also for the overall health of the global ecosystem.

Indigenous knowledge and traditional practices can provide valuable insights into sustainable living in the Arctic. Indigenous communities have thrived in this harsh environment for thousands of years, using time-tested methods of hunting, fishing, and resource management. Incorporating Indigenous perspectives into decision-making processes can ensure that sustainable practices respect cultural heritage and traditional ways of life.

One of the most critical aspects of preserving the Arctic for future generations is addressing the concerns and rights of Indigenous communities. Recognizing and respecting Indigenous sovereignty and self-determination is crucial in shaping sustainable policies and avoiding the mistakes of past colonial practices.

In addition to environmental and social considerations, responsible tourism and responsible business practices are also essential for a sustainable Arctic future. Sustainable tourism promotes ecotourism and cultural experiences that do not harm the environment or exploit local communities. Responsible businesses must prioritize ethical practices, support local economies, and minimize their ecological footprint.

Education and public awareness are powerful tools in shaping a sustainable future for the Arctic. By raising awareness of the region's unique challenges and highlighting the importance of conservation, we can inspire action and advocacy at both individual and collective levels.

Epilogue

As we conclude our journey through the Arctic, we are left with a profound appreciation for the beauty, complexity, and fragility of this vast and enchanting region. The Arctic is not just a remote and frozen wilderness; it is a place of immense significance to our planet and our collective future.

Throughout this book, we have explored the rich tapestry of the Arctic's history, culture, wildlife, and environment. We have delved into the stories of ancient civilizations and the traditions of Indigenous peoples who have called this land home for thousands of years. We have marveled at the majestic polar bears, the agile Arctic foxes, and the graceful Arctic birds that have adapted to survive in this extreme environment.

We have witnessed the effects of climate change, with the melting ice and rising temperatures transforming the Arctic at an alarming rate. The consequences of these changes extend far beyond the Arctic's borders, affecting weather patterns, sea levels, and ecosystems around the world.

In our exploration of Arctic diplomacy, we have seen the importance of international cooperation and responsible governance in addressing the challenges and opportunities presented by the changing Arctic. We have recognized the value of Indigenous knowledge and the need to respect the rights and perspectives of Arctic communities in shaping policies and practices.

As we contemplate the future of the Arctic, we are faced with critical choices that will determine the fate of this unique and delicate ecosystem. The quest for energy resources, the push for economic development, and the allure of Arctic tourism must be balanced with the imperative to protect and preserve this pristine wilderness for future generations.

The Arctic is not just a distant and isolated region; it is a part of our shared global heritage. The choices we make today will reverberate across the Arctic and the world, shaping the destiny of this frozen frontier and impacting the lives of those who call it home.

Our journey through the Arctic has taught us that we are all interconnected, and the health of the Arctic is inseparable from the health of our planet. As we confront the challenges of climate change and environmental degradation, we are reminded of the responsibility we bear to safeguard the Arctic and its inhabitants.

In the end, the Arctic is a symbol of both vulnerability and resilience. It is a call to action, urging us to come together as global citizens to protect this precious corner of the world and ensure a sustainable future for generations to come.

As we bid farewell to the Arctic, let us carry its lessons with us, cherishing the wonders of nature, embracing the wisdom of Indigenous cultures, and committing ourselves to be stewards of this magnificent and fragile region. The Arctic is a place of wonder, awe, and inspiration, and its fate is intertwined with our own. May we rise to the challenge and stand together to preserve the Arctic for the generations that will follow, ensuring that its beauty and majesty endure for all time.

Printed in Great Britain
by Amazon